Connecting Comics to Curriculum

Connecting Comics to Curriculum

Strategies for Grades 6–12

Karen W. Gavigan and Mindy Tomasevich

LIBRARIES UNLIMITED

AN IMPRINT OF ABC-CLIO, LLC
Santa Barbara, California • Denver, Colorado • Oxford, England

Library of Congress Cataloging-in-Publication Data

Gavigan, Karen W.
   Connecting comics to curriculum : strategies for grades 6–12 / Karen W. Gavigan and Mindy Tomasevich.
      p. cm.
   Includes bibliographical references and index.
   ISBN 978–1–59884–768–0 (pbk.) — ISBN 978–1–59884–769–7 (ebook)   1. Comic books, strips, etc., in education. 2. Graphic novels in education. 3. Middle school education—Activity programs—United States. 4. Education, Secondary—Activity programs—United States. 5. Libraries—Special collections—Comic books, strips, etc. 6. Libraries—Special collections—Graphic novels. 7. Comic books, strips, etc.—Bibliography. 8. Graphic novels—Bibliography. I. Tomasevich, Mindy. II. Title.
LB1044.9.C59G38   2011
372.6'044—dc23   2011029009

ISBN: 978–1–59884–768–0
EISBN: 978–1–59884–769–7

15 14 13 12 11   1 2 3 4 5

This book is also available on the World Wide Web as an eBook.
Visit www.abc-clio.com for details.

Libraries Unlimited
An Imprint of ABC-CLIO, LLC

ABC-CLIO, LLC
130 Cremona Drive, P.O. Box 1911
Santa Barbara, California 93116-1911

This book is printed on acid-free paper (∞)
Manufactured in the United States of America

Copyright Acknowledgments

Excerpts from *Standards for the 21st-Century Learner* by the American Association of School Librarians, a division of the American Library Association, copyright © 2007 American Library Association. Available for download at www.ala.org/aasl/standards. Used with permission.

Standards for the English Language Arts, by the International Reading Association and the National Council of Teachers of English, Copyright 1996 by the International Reading Association and the National Council of Teachers of English. Reprinted with permission. Available online at http://www.ncte.org/standards.

Excerpts from *The National Standards for Arts Education*, © 1994 by MENC: The National Association for Music Education. Reprinted with permission.

Contents

Foreword

As the volume you hold in your hands or are reading on a digital device shows, sequential art (comics) as an educational tool has finally come of age. For the past sixty-plus years, comics were often considered useless children's drivel with little or no value. Certainly in many educational and librarian circles they were looked down upon as being the literary equivalent of smelly trash to be discarded. During the late 1940s and early 1950s, comics were argued to be one of the causes of juvenile delinquency (similar arguments in recent years have been leveled at movies, television, video games, popular music, and the Internet). Nevertheless, there were also those forward-looking sequential art artists and writers (along with educators and librarians) who stood up to argue that perhaps the format could be used to convey content beyond the "juvenile fantasy" story. As early as 1928 with the publication of the graphic novel "prototype," *Texas History Movies*, the format has been used to convey content that enlightens as well as entertains. (Need I mention the *Classics Illustrated* series through which many a youth was exposed through the sequential art format to the basic storyline of the world's great literature? *Classics Illustrated* also produced historical and scientific comics in an attempt to provide a worthwhile alternative to other types of comics). In the last several decades, we've seen the work of folks like Larry Gonick and Patrick Reynolds, as well as the *For Beginners* and *Introducing* series, use sequential art to teach everything from world history, physics, and mathematics to the complicated ideas of notable philosophers and scientists like Stephen Hawking, Wilhelm Reich, and Michel Foucault.

Although one still might find a few naysayers who would question the validity of sequential art in the classroom, fortunately for most educators this is not an issue. A better question might be, "Just which graphic novels should we use?" So many choices exist now. It is an exciting time to be an educator who uses graphic novels in the classroom. Literally hundreds of graphic novels are published to educate as well as entertain. Thankfully, Karen W. Gavigan and Mindy Tomasevich show us in *Connecting Comics to Curriculum: Strategies for Grades 6–12*, that educators can use comics as a way to entice not only reluctant readers, but all readers.

Gavigan and Tomasevich provide a wealth of practical advice, lesson plans, and suggest selected graphic novels to teach specific content. This volume is a godsend for teachers and librarians, covering how to incorporate sequential art into every aspect of the educational experience from teaching writing, history, and the fine arts, to social sciences as well as hard science. They don't leave out the popular form of manga or how to build up a core collection of graphic novels for students to peruse. One of the things I continually harp on is that you use both sides of your brain when reading comics (right side to interpret the sequential images and left side to interpret the narrative). Thus reading comics might actually make you smarter. I can't tell you how many people have come up to me to say that they learned to read by first reading comics. Getting young people "hooked" on comics is a great way to instill a love of reading that goes on well into adulthood. With all of the sequential-art-based movies, video games, television shows, and toys pervading popular culture, it only makes sense to incorporate graphic novels into your curriculum. Luckily, *Connecting Comics to Curriculum: Strategies for Grades 6–12* shows us how to do that successfully. Did I mention this can be fun for the instructors as well? Go forth and use this volume as a guide to give your students an educational experience they will never forget!

Robert G. Weiner
Texas Tech University Library

Robert G. Weiner is associate Humanities Librarian for Texas Tech University. He is the editor of Graphic Novels in Libraries and Archives *and author of* Marvel Graphic Novels: An Annotated Guide. *He is also on the editorial board for the* Journal of Graphic Novel and Comics. *While working as a public librarian, Weiner helped build an expansive graphic novel collection including designing a unique in-house cataloging system. Weiner's work with graphic novels at the public library was published in two separate articles in* Texas Library Journal *(2002, 2008).*

Acknowledgments

I would like to acknowledge the support and encouragement of my husband, Frank Gavigan, my sons, John and Matt, my parents, John and Pat Weyher, and my sister, Melissa Saunders. I also would like to express my appreciation to Robin Brenner, Sterg Botzakis, and Rob Weiner for sharing their expertise. A special thank you goes to Meredith Keeter, Graduate Assistant Extraordinaire.

—Karen

Writing this book would not have been possible without the unending support of my husband, Mark, my children, John and Anne, and my parents, Jan and Bill Hughes, as well as the generous assistance of Wanda Johnson, Jan Kidd, Adrian Phillips, Anne Tomasevich, Kathy Vincent, and Jill Zappia.

—Mindy

We would both like to thank Debbie Dupree, Michele Gorman, Zena Harvley-Felder, Gerry Solomon, and especially Sharon Coatney, our editor, for their assistance and support.

Introduction

Whether you are a novice when it comes to graphic novels or an *otaku* (a Japanese term for people obsessed with manga), this book is for you. If you are just getting started with graphic novels, you will learn about recommended lists of titles and practical advice on using them with students in grades 6–12. In addition to definitions and the elements of graphic novels, you will find a summary of recent publishing trends, awards, and recognitions. If you are a graphic novel aficionado, you will learn how to use curriculum-based graphic novels in your library or classroom. If you are already sold on graphic novels but have administrators, teachers, patrons, and/or parents who question their merit, this book will introduce you to the growing body of research that validates their use in schools and libraries. There are suggested hands-on activities you can use to share graphic novels with teachers and students. In addition to selective lists of graphic novel titles for secondary students, you will find a bibliography of professional titles and a list of helpful websites. Whatever your level of expertise, this book will provide you with innovative ideas and standards-based lesson plans you can use in your libraries and classrooms. So get ready to discover some proven ideas for using graphic novels in your libraries and classrooms. Soon graphic novels will be leaping off of your shelves in a single bound.

Chapter 1

Comics and Curriculum: Getting Started with Graphic Novels

Imagine these scenes in a school or public library: students heading straight for the graphic novel collection, sitting on the floor and examining books they have pulled from the shelves, browsing through graphic novels at tables, and sharing titles with each other. What exactly are they doing?

- A middle school student is looking for a graphic novel biography, or collective biography, of a scientist to prepare a report for science class.
- Several middle school students are talking about the latest volumes of their favorite manga series.
- A high school boy is reading a graphic novel adaptation of *Macbeth* to help him comprehend the dialogue for his AP English Language Arts class.
- A high school girl is at the circulation desk checking out the title *Inside Out: Portrait of an Eating Disorder* (Shivack, 2007) to help her understand a classmate's struggle with bulimia.
- Two high school English Language Learner (ELL) students are examining a copy of *The United States Constitution: A Graphic Adaptation* (Hennessey and McConnell, 2008) to prepare for their next U.S. History class.

Would you like to see this type of interest in reading from middle and high school students in your library and classroom? You can, when you provide them with access to a wide variety of fiction and nonfiction graphic novel titles. However, getting your students engaged in reading graphic novels requires more than providing access. You need strategies for using graphic novels to meet your students' recreational and informational needs. You need lists of graphic novel titles and ideas for using them across the curriculum with readers who have a wide range of abilities. Finally, you need to know what type of student and patron you are serving.

Take a look around at today's adolescents. Whether texting, tweeting, listening to music, or sending photos to friends, they are making connections and processing information using both text and images. To reach these twenty-first century learners, librarians and teachers must understand and teach visual literacies in today's classrooms

1

and libraries. These young people have grown up in a mediasphere world filled with visual images such as the Internet, television, and video games; they eagerly embrace multimodal formats that combine visuals with text. Graphic novels use an arrangement of art, and thought and speech balloons that is familiar to today's visually literate students. They also fulfill a wide range of students' reading interests, whether it is through middle school students reading about the story of an Iranian girl's childhood in *Persepolis* (Satrapi, 2003), students in Advanced Placement (AP) classes reading about the Holocaust via *Maus* (Spiegelman, 1992), or struggling adolescent readers enjoying the familiarity of Jeff Smith's *Bone* series. Yet, many librarians and teachers are still not comfortable including graphic novels in their libraries and classrooms. For those who are not familiar with graphic novels, an introduction to the format is provided.

Graphic Novels 101

Before you begin adding graphic novels to your library or classroom, you must first understand what they are. The following list of definitions will help you comprehend the multimodal world of graphic novels, manga, and anime.

Graphic novel—An original book-length story, either fiction or nonfiction, published in comic book style, or a collection of stories that have been published previously as individual comic books (Gorman, 2003). Graphic novel refers to a format and not a genre. All genres such as biography, science fiction, historical non-fiction, fantasy, and so on can be subjects for graphic novels.

Manga *(mawn-guh)*—The Japanese word for comic book. A Japanese format consisting of comic books and graphic novels, typically black-and-white, and featuring stylized characters with large, round eyes. Manga titles read from back to front and right to left. They are usually published in a series in the following gender-based categories:

- *Shôjo—young teenage girls*
- *Shônen—young teenage boys*. Although *shônen* titles are typically written for boys, they have a crossover appeal for many girls as well.

Anime *(AH-nee-may)*—An abbreviated Japanese pronunciation of "animation." Graphic novel titles are often based on anime productions. They are cartoon animations available via television broadcasts, video, and online. Anime productions are characterized by bright graphics and action-filled plots, often with Ninja, fantasy, and futuristic themes.

Sequential Art—An art form that features a series of images in a sequence to tell a story or convey information. The most common formats of sequential art are comic books, comic strips, and graphic novels.

Visual literacy—The act of making meaning, using still or moving images, through visual formats such as graphic novels, manga, anime, and so on. A visually literate person understands how images contribute to the meaning of the whole.

A great first step in learning about visual literacy is to read *Understanding Comics* by Scott McCloud (1994). McCloud's informative book, a graphic novel in itself, provides an engaging look at graphic novel elements and an overview of the format. Some of the graphic novel elements that McCloud refers to in his book are listed in the sidebar.

Yet, even with an understanding of the format, many librarians and teachers are reluctant to include graphic novel titles in their collections and lesson plans. It may be because of their own reluctance, or because of the influence of others who have discouraged the use of graphic novels in schools and libraries. To dispel any fears about using graphic novels with children and young adults, and to learn about some proven success stories, it is helpful to examine the current body of graphic novel research.

Elements of Graphic Novels

Bleed—text and illustrations that run to the edge of a page

Captions—contain information about a scene or a character, and are generally used to establish the time and setting of a story

Gutters—the space between borders

Motion Lines—motion lines, or action lines, refer to the abstract lines that appear behind a moving object or person to make them look like they are moving quickly

Panels—squares or rectangles that contain text and illustrations from a single scene

Panel frames—the border or edges of a panel

Sound effects—presented within balloons, usually in all capital letters

Speech bubbles, or word balloons—the balloon that represents the speech of a character spoken aloud

Symbolia—iconic representations used within comics and cartooning. Examples include the use of a light bulb over a character's head to indicate an idea, or the use of "zzzz" to indicate sleep.

Thought balloons—the balloon that conveys the thoughts of a character

What the Research Says

To understand the importance of including graphic novels in your library collections, it is necessary to have an understanding of the body of research and theory examining their use with children and adolescents. Several years ago, there was little research regarding the use of graphic novels in schools and libraries. Fortunately, there have been a growing number of such studies in recent years. These studies can be helpful in convincing naysayers of the value of using graphic novels with diverse populations of students. For example, some studies have shown that graphic novels can motivate readers to achieve reading enjoyment and success (Botzakis, 2009; Carter, 2007; Hammond, 2009; Monnin, 2008). There are many educators and theorists who believe that graphic novels can help make the curriculum more relevant for our students (Alvermann and Xu, 2003; Schwarz, 2002; Xu, Sawyer, and Zunich, 2005). Additional studies have examined the use of graphic novels with specific populations of students.

Boys and Male Adolescents

Reports on achievement scores in the United States consistently indicate that boys are being outperformed by girls in the area of reading (Tyre, 2006). In the 1990s, the

During a lesson on sequential art, these middle school boys share their enthusiasm for graphic novels.

U.S. Department of Education estimated that "the gap in reading proficiency between males and females (favoring girls) is roughly equivalent to about one and one half years of school" for seventeen-year-old students (National Center for Education Statistics [NCES], 1995). Fortunately, several studies have shown that when male readers select engaging reading materials, such as graphic novels, it can help them find their reading voices by choosing to read rather than choosing not to read at all (Brozo, 2002; Ivey and Fisher, 2006; Krashen, 2004). For example, a study by Ujiie and Krashen (1996) examined the comic book reading of 571 seventh-graders at two California middle schools. Although half of the girls reported that they did not read comics, 83 percent of the boys indicated that they always, or sometimes, read comic books. A little over half of these comic-book readers reported that they liked to read, as opposed to 21 percent of the non-comic-book readers. In addition, in a longitudinal study of male reading habits, Smith & Wilhelm (2002) found that graphic novels were one of the few types of texts that actively engaged male readers. Similarly, a Canadian study revealed that males respond positively to images, because they are more oriented to visual/spatial learning (Ontario Ministry of Education, 2004).

English Language Learners

Recently, graphic novel studies have focused on the use of graphic novels with English Language Learners (ELL) (Cary, 2004; Chun, 2009; Liu, 2004; Ranker, 2007). These studies found that the high interest topics and visual support found in graphic novels were beneficial to ELL students. For example, Cary's 2004 study demonstrated that graphic novels include authentic dialogue that can help English Language Learners comprehend everyday English.

Special Needs Students

Other recent studies have demonstrated the value of using graphic novels with special needs students (Smetana, Odelson, Burns, and Grisham, 2009; Young and Irwin, 2005). For example, Young and Irwin (2005) worked with students in special education classes to determine whether or not graphic novels can improve reading outcomes, motivate students to read more, and enhance student achievement. They found that students could visualize text after reading graphic novels, and that some of the previous non-readers became readers once they were introduced to the graphic novel format. Similarly, Smetana et al. (2009) found that graphic novels were a valuable format for engaging failing deaf students in a remedial summer school course. The combination of text and visuals helped to scaffold the students' understanding of literacy skills.

The academic needs of struggling male readers, English Language Learners, and special needs students are an ongoing concern for librarians, teachers, and parents. Because of the documented potential for connecting these students to graphic novels, there is a growing demand for curriculum-based strategies for using graphic novels in libraries and classrooms. Given that, "A less motivated reader spends less time reading, exerts lower cognitive effort, and is less dedicated to full comprehension than a more highly motivated reader" (Guthrie and Wigfield, 2000, p. 406), the popularity of graphic novels has promising implications for the reading motivation and achievement of marginalized readers.

Additional Research and Theory

Several educators and theorists have described further educational and social benefits of using graphic novels with students. For example, Burmark (2002) writes that the most compelling reason for using visuals in the classroom is that images are stored in long-term memory, which aids comprehension. Visualization is often recommended as a literacy teaching strategy, because images can be used to facilitate students' reading comprehension. The visuals in graphic novels make the text less threatening and can help to increase engagement and motivation (Gorman, 2003; Krashen, 2004; Lyga, 2004). The wide range of texts and storylines in graphic novels is appealing to students who may have difficulty reading linguistic text (Wilber, 2008). In addition, other literacy researchers have found that graphic novels can be used effectively to teach multiple literacies (Carter, 2007, Carter and Evensen, 2011; Frey and Fisher, 2008; Schwarz, 2002).

In his book, *Developing and Promoting Graphic Novel Collections*, Miller (2005, pp. 29–30) lists some of the following reasons for using graphic novels in educational settings:

1. Graphic novels can help students develop literacy and language skills by reinforcing vocabulary.
2. Graphic novels offer students a chance to explore visual literacy and develop critical thinking skills.
3. Graphic novels can present information about literature, history, and social issues in ways that appeal to reluctant readers.
4. Graphic novels provide stepping stones to full-text classics and spring boards to extra learning activities.
5. Graphic novels can inspire challenged students who lack reading confidence, reading ability, or motivation for self-guided reading.

Mitchell and George (1996) maintain that comics are effective tools for teaching gifted children about morals and ethics. Similarly, Schwarz (2002) found that an important benefit of using graphic novels is their ability to present alternative views of culture, history, and human life. For example, graphic novels can be used to address relevant social issues, such as bullying and divorce. Consider, for example, *Yummy* (Neri and Duburke, 2009), a graphic novel depicting the true story of gang-related violence in south-side Chicago.

Librarians and teachers are recognizing that one way to motivate students to read is to provide them with the ability to choose more varied and interesting reading materials, such as graphic novels. Cary (2004) found that the non-traditional, visual format of graphic novels consistently engaged readers through elements such as humor, heroes, and art. Others see the value of using graphic novels with twenty-first-century learners. In the words of Gene Yang, author of *American Born Chinese* (2006), "Comics is a multimedia medium. It is a single medium made up of two distinct media: still images and text. When students learn to read comics, and especially when they learn to create comics, they're learning this twenty-first-century skill of making decisions about information, and about media" (Standen, 2010). Other studies support the view that reading light materials, such as comics and graphic novels, is the way many reluctant readers develop a taste for reading and can lead to the reading of other, more traditional texts (Krashen, 2004). For example, Haugaard (1973) reported that her eldest son, an avid comic reader, gave his comic collection to his younger brother when he became more interested in reading the likes of ". . . Jules Verne and Ray Bradbury, books on electronics, and science encyclopedias" (p. 85). Furthermore, the results of a study of seventh-grade boys showed that reading comics did not inhibit other kinds of reading (Ujiie and Krashen, 1996). Frey and Fisher (2004, 2008) found that the visuals in graphic novels enable students to have positive reading experiences, which makes them more likely to want to read more.

Circulation data from public and school libraries indicate that reading graphic novels can stimulate readers' interest in additional reading materials (Brenner, 2009). For instance, some libraries have reported 25 percent increases in overall collection circulation after adding graphic novels to their collections (Miller, 2005). Allison Steinberg, a school librarian in California, increased her library circulation by 50 percent after purchasing $1,000 worth of graphic novels (*Curriculum Review*, 2004).

Publishing Trends

The number of graphic novels published each year has grown exponentially in the last decade, as graphic novel publishing companies have added graphic novel lines, or imprints, to their publishing houses. Other non-comic publishers are creating graphic novel presses to meet the growing demands of today's readers. For example, Capstone launched its graphic novel division, *Graphic Libraries* in 2005. In the same year, Scholastic created its own graphic novel imprint, *Graphix*. To meet the growing demands of its readers, the publishing industry is releasing graphic novels representing a variety of genres, subjects, and social issues. As additional genres have become available, the market has responded. Overall, graphic novel sales in the United States and Canada for 2008 were $395 million (*Publishers Weekly*, Feb. 2009). In 2007 graphic novel sales in the United States and Canada were \$375 million, a 12% rise from 2006 and quintuple the sales number from 2001 (MacDonald, 2009). In terms of K-12 graphic novel sales, over 4 million graphic novels were sold at Scholastic Book Fairs from 2004–2007 (Reed Business Information, 2007).

Awards and Recognition

The popularity of graphic novels grew in leaps and bounds after 1992, when Art Spiegelman was awarded the Pulitzer-Prize for his comic book memoir, *Maus: A Survivor's Tale*. When Spiegelman received the award, it helped to establish the graphic novel's legitimacy in the literary world. The rapid growth of graphic novel publications and sales has been followed by an increasing recognition of their literary merit for all ages and on a variety of topics. For example, Judd Winick (2000) won numerous awards for *Pedro and Me*, an autobiographical graphic novel about his friendship with AIDS educator Pedro Zamora after the two met while on a reality television series. The book's awards included the Robert F. Sibert Informational Book Honor Award (2001), as well as the American Library Association's Notable Children's Book Selection (2001). Later, *American Born Chinese* (Yang, 2006) won the 2007 Michael L. Printz Award for a book that exemplifies literary excellence in young adult literature. In the book, Yang alternates three interrelated stories about the problems of young Chinese Americans trying to participate in the popular culture. The title was also on the list of the 2007 Top Ten Best Books for Young Adults (YALSA), and it was a 2006 National Book Award Finalist in the Young People's Literature Category.

In 2007, the Young Adult Library Services Association (YALSA) created an annual list of award-winning graphic novels for adolescents, Great Graphic Novels for Teens. This annual list, of recommended graphic novels and illustrated nonfiction for adolescents, has helped to shine a spotlight on quality graphic novels for libraries and schools. Additional awards for graphic novels for adolescents include:

- 2007 Printz Honor award for *To Dance* (Siegel, 2006), an autobiographical memoir about a ballerina
- 2010 Scott O'Dell Award for historical fiction for *Storm in the Barn* (Phelan, 2009), a story about the Dust Bowl
- *Yummy* (Neri and Duburke) was named the 2010 Coretta Scott King Author Honor Award, 2010 ALA Notable Book, a 2010 Great Graphic Novel for Teens, and a YALSA Top Ten Quick Pick for Reluctant Readers.

Using Graphic Novels across the Curriculum

Students may become more willing to engage in reading across the curriculum when librarians and teachers allow them to use nontraditional texts, such as graphic novels, that they are motivated to read. As Gurian (2005) writes, textbooks "may not be engaging enough to keep boys (or girls) interested" (p. 140). Graphic novels can supplement textbooks and provide many learners with the support they need to comprehend course content. Furthermore, the large assortment of storylines and information represent a variety of curriculum areas, and meet the diverse reading needs of students. As Frey and Fisher (2008, p. 103) found, "this medium (graphic novels) ful-fills a wide range of our students reading interests."

Hopefully, now that you are familiar with research that validates the use of graphic novels in schools and libraries, you are ready to begin developing a graphic novel collection. If you already have graphic novels in your library or classroom, you may want to learn some tips for developing an even better collection. Yet, how do you know what titles to buy? What are some criteria for purchasing titles? Where do you begin? Chapter 2 provides you with the information you need to answer all of these questions, and more.

References

Alvermann, Donna E., and Shirley H. Xu. Children's Everyday Literacies: Intersections of Popular Culture and Language Arts Instruction. *Language Arts. 81*(2), 145–54, 2003, November.

Botzakis, Sterg. Graphic Novels in Education: Cartoons, Comprehension, and Content Knowl-edge. In Deborah Wooten, & Bernice Cullinan (Eds.), *Children's Literature in the Reading Program* (pp. 15–23). Newark, DE: International Reading Association, 2009.

Brozo, William G. *To Be a Boy, To Be a Reader: Engaging Teen and Preteen Boys in Active Literacy.* Newark: DE: International Reading Association, 2002.

Brenner, Robin. Number Crunching: How Looking at Graphic novel Circulation Statistics from Many Perspectives Help You Know What's Really Flying off the Shelves. Retrieved from http://blog.schoollibraryjournal.com/goodcomicsforkids/2009/11/21/number-crunching -how-looking-at-graphic-novel-circulation-statistics-from-many-perspectives-help-you -know-whats-really-flying-off-the-shelves, 2009.

Burmark, Lynell. *Visual literacy: Learn to see, see to learn.* Alexandria, VA: ASCD Publications, 2002.

Carter, J. Bucky. *Building Literacy Connections with Graphic Novels: Page by Page, Panel by Panel.* National Council of Teachers of English, 2007.

Carter, J. Bucky, and Erik Evensen. *Super-powered Word Study: Teaching Words and Word Parts through Comics.* Gainesville, FL: Maupin House Pub, 2011.

Cary, Stephen. *Going graphic: Comics at Work in the Multilingual Classroom.* Portsmouth, NH: Heinemann, 2004.

Chun, C. W. (2009, October). Critical Literacies and Graphic Novels for English-Language Learners: Teaching *Maus. Journal of Adolescent & Adult Literacy, 53,* 144–53.

Curriculum Review. Adding comic books leads to circulation gains. 44 (1), 1–3, 2004.

Frey, Nancy, and Doug Fisher. *Teaching Visual Literacy: Using Comic Books, Graphic Novels, Anime, Cartoons, and More to Develop Comprehension and Thinking Skills.* Thousand Oaks, CA: Corwin Press, 2008.

Frey, Nancy, and Fisher, Doug, Using Graphic Novels, Anime, and the Internet in an Urban High School. *English Journal, 93*(3), 19–25, 2004.

Gorman, Michele. *Getting graphic! Using Graphic Novels to Promote Literacy with Pre-teens and Teens.* Worthington, OH: Linworth Publishing, Inc., 2003.

Gurian, Michael, and Kathy Stevens. *The Minds of Boys: Saving our Sons From Falling Behind in School and Life.* San Francisco, CA: Jossey Bass, 2005.

Guthrie, John T., and Allan Wigfield. Engagement and Motivation in Reading. In Michael L. Kamil, Peter B. Mosenthal, P. David Pearson, & Rebecca Barr (Eds.), *Handbook of reading research* (Vol. III, pp. 403–22). Mahwah, NJ: Lawrence Erlbaum, 2000.

Hammond, Heidi. *Graphic Novels and Multimodal Literacy: A Reader Response Study*. Ph.D. dissertation, University of Minnesota, United States—Minnesota. Retrieved February 3, 2010, from Dissertations & Theses: Full Text. (Publication No. AAT 3344687), 2009.

Haugaard, Kay. Comic Books: A Conduit to Culture? *Reading Teacher, 27,* 54–55, 1973.

Hennessey, Jonathan, and Aaron McConnell. *The United States Constitution: A Graphic Adaptation*, New York: Hill and Wang, 2008.

Ivey, Gay, and Doug Fisher. Creating Literacy-Rich Schools for Adolescents. Alexandria, VA: Association for Supervision and Curriculum Development, 2006.

Krashen, Stephen. *The Power of Reading: Insights from the Research*. Second Edition. Portsmouth, NH: Libraries Unlimited, 2004.

Krashen, Stephen, and Joanne Ujiie. Is Comic Book Reading Harmful? Comic Book Reading, School Achievement, and Pleasure Reading Among Seventh Graders. *California School Library Association Journal, 19,* 27–28. 1996.

Liu, Jun. Effects of Comic Strips on L2 Learners' Reading Comprehension. *TESOL Quarterly, 38,* 225–43, 2004.

Lyga, Allyson W. & Lyga, Barry *Graphic Novels in Your Media Center: A Definitive Guide*. Westport, CT: Libraries Unlimited, 2004.

McCloud, Scott. *Understanding Comics*. Northampton, MA: Kitchen Sink Press, 1993.

Miller, Stephen. *Developing and Promoting Graphic Novel Collections*. New York: Neal-Schuman Publishers, 2005.

Mitchell, J. P., and George, J. D. What do Superman, Captain America, and Spiderman have in common? The case for comic books. *Gifted Education International, 11,* 91–94, 1996.

Monnin, Katie. *Perceptions of New Literacies with the Graphic Novel "Bone."* Ph.D. Dissertation. Kent State University, 2008.

National Center for Education Statistics. *The Condition of Education*, 1995. Washington, DC: U.S. Department of Education, 1995.

Neri, Greg, and Randy DuBurke. *Yummy: the Last Days of a Southside Shorty*. New York: Lee & Low Books, 2010.

Ontario Ministry of Education. *Me Read? No way! A practical guide to Improving Boys' Literacy Skills*. Ontario: Queen's Printer for Ontario. Retrieved October 11, 2005 from www.edu.gov.on.ca, 2004.

Ranker, Jason. Using Comic Books as Read-Alouds: Insights on Reading Instruction from an English as a Second Language Classroom. *Reading Teacher, 61,* 296–305, 2007.

Satrapi, Marjane. *Persepolis*. New York: Pantheon Books, 2003.

Schwarz, Gretchen E. Graphic Novels for Multiple Literacies. *Journal of Adolescent & Adult Literacy, 46* (3), 262–65, 2002.

Shivack, Nadia. *Inside Out: Portrait of an Eating Disorder*. New York: Ginee Seo Books, 2007.

Smetana, Linda, Dara Odelson, Heidi Burns, and Dana Grisham. Using Graphic Novels in the High School Classroom: Engaging Deaf Students with a New Genre. *Journal of Adolescent & Adult Literacy, 53,* 228–40. Retrieved from ERIC database, 2009.

Smith, Michael W., and Jeffrey D. Wilhelm. *"Reading Don't Fix No Chevy's": Literacy in the Lives of Young Men*. Portsmouth, NH: Heinemann, 2002.

Spiegelman, Art. *Maus: A Survivor's Tale*. New York: Pantheon Books, 1986.

Standen, Amy. My Life in comics: A Math Teacher Draws on His Experiences. Edutopia.org. The George Lucas Foundation. Retrieved February 18, 2011 from http://www.edutopia.org/comic-books-american-born-chinese. 2010.

Tyre, Peg. The Trouble with Boys. *Newsweek, 5,* 44–52, 2006, January 30.

Ujiie, Joanne, and Stephen Krashen. Comic Book Reading, Reading Enjoyment, and Pleasure reading among Middle Class and Chapter 1 Middle School Students. *Reading Improvement*, 33, 41–54, 1996, Spring.

Winnick, Judd. *Pedro and Me: Friendship, Loss, and What I Learned*. New York: Henry Holt and Company, 2000.

Xu, Shirley H., Sawyer, Rachel W., and Zunich, Lark O. *Trading Cards to Comic Strips: Popular Culture Texts and Literacy Learning in Grades K-8*. Newark, DE: International Reading Association, 2005.

Yang, Gene L. *American Born Chinese*. New York: Roaring Brook Press, 2006.

Young, Robyn, and Marilyn Irwin. *Graphic Novels Boost Interest in Reading among Students with Disabilities*. Indiana University | Purdue University | IUPU Columbus (2006). Retrieved May 6, 2009 from www.iupui.edu/news/releases/050906_graphic_novels.htm

Chapter 2

Criteria, Curriculum, and Conundrums

Deciding which graphic novels to buy for your library or school can seem like a daunting task. If you are a beginner, these books appear very different from fiction or nonfiction materials you may usually purchase. Not only is the format unique—with panels and sequential art on every page—a vast variety of stories and styles are also available. Manga, with its Japanese influence and pages that flow in a direction unfamiliar to many, can be especially puzzling to the uninitiated. And, with so many new titles published each year, even if you are used to purchasing graphic novels, you may become overwhelmed by all the choices.

This chapter will give you the tools and knowledge you need to confidently select graphic novels for your library or classroom. You will learn how to evaluate graphic novels, where to locate professional reviews, and which titles might be outstanding choices for your own patrons and students. You will be on your way to becoming an expert. But first, to demystify the task of selecting graphic novels, take a moment to compare it to something you already do, and probably do quite well.

How do you choose which books to add to your library or classroom? Most likely, you have procedures you follow. These procedures are set by your library system or school district in the form of a collection development and management policy. A written policy sets forth processes to follow when selecting and procuring library books, textbooks, periodicals, multimedia, software—everything. It sets standards of equity and access, gives criteria to use when evaluating materials, and ensures that standardized guidelines are followed. You are probably very familiar with it, and if you have been making purchases for a library or school for very long, you follow it as second nature. A formal collection development and management policy does not only help you make decisions; it provides you with insurance, too. By following the policy and making informed, thoughtful choices, you will be prepared if objections arise. If a parent, staff member, or patron questions a book or other resource in the library or school, you will be asked at some point why you acquired that item. If you've followed the policy, you can easily explain your choice and how it meets the needs of the wide variety of patrons and students your library or school serves. Though it is impossible to avoid all controversy, most librarians and teachers are comfortable working within

The Bottom Line

Don't despair—selecting graphic novels is similar to the selection of other materials.

a collection development and management policy, and appreciate the help it offers when making choices.

The good news is that graphic novels should fall under the same collection development and management policy you already use. Some policies mention them specifically; others incorporate them through all-inclusive terminology (Goldsmith, 2005). You will choose graphic novels in the same way you choose other books, by:

- Reading reviews
- Looking at lists of recommended titles
- Determining which books fill reading and curricular needs
- Considering age and developmental appropriateness
- Using criteria to evaluate content, writing, art, authoritativeness, and accuracy

This chapter will describe in detail how to select and evaluate graphic novels, and point you in the right direction to find reviews and lists of recommended titles—all the tools you will need to choose the best graphic novels for the adolescents at your library or school.

Reviews Sources

These days it is easy to find reviews of graphic novels. Beginning in the mid-1990s, library journals and mainstream library periodicals began reviewing graphic novels (Goldsmith, 2005; Miller, 2005), and websites have sprung up that include reviews by both professional reviewers and graphic novel readers. Many of the resources you may already use include graphic novels among the books they regularly review. A list of some of these review sources is provided in the sidebar.

Lists of Suggested Titles

This book includes many lists of graphic novel titles suggested for middle and high school–aged students. The chapters pertaining to specific subject areas include lists of titles that cover those areas of the curriculum. Also included are lists of manga titles, books featuring superheroes, and, in Appendixes 1 and 2, core lists of suggested titles for librarians and teachers who are just starting a collection or who want to improve an existing one.

Many authors of professional development books about graphic novels have included their own lists and issues for librarians and teachers to consider, and you can find a bibliography of some of these professional resources at the end of this chapter. There are inherent problems with any list of graphic novel titles, however. Graphic novels, sometimes even acclaimed titles, tend to go out of print fairly quickly (Goldsmith, 2005). Popularity changes rapidly, too, and what is in high demand now may languish on the shelf in no time. Considering both "golden oldies" as well as current top-sellers is a way to be certain your collection will provide continuous appeal.

Most of the online resources mentioned in this book also contain lists of titles recommended for purchase. Graphic novel publishers, book vendors, and jobbers compile lists of titles they recommend, often broken down by grade level or age. It is especially easy to find end-of-year compilations in journals and on websites that list the best graphic novels of the year.

As mentioned in Chapter 1, an invaluable resource for selecting recently published graphic novels is The Young Adult Library Services Association's (YALSA) Great Graphic Novels for Teens lists. Each year a YALSA committee evaluates nominated titles—both fiction and nonfiction—and publishes a list of the best graphic novels for adolescents aged 12 to 18. These lists can be found at http://www.ala.org/yalsa/ggnt.

The Will Eisner Comic Industry Awards are given annually to graphic novels in dozens of categories, including several for children and adolescents. A committee creates lists of nominees, and winners are chosen by professionals from all areas of the comics industry. Lists of Eisner Award winners can be found at http://www.comic-con.org/cci/cci_eisners_pastwinners.php. Similarly, the Harvey Awards are given each year to comic creators and their works, as voted on by others in the profession, and many graphic novels written for children and adolescents have been

Print Resources for Graphic Novel Reviews

- *Booklist* and *Book Links*
- *The Horn Book*
- *Bulletin of the Center for Children's Books*
- *Library Journal*
- *Library Media Connection*
- *The New York Times*
- *Publisher's Weekly*
- *School Library Journal*
- *Teacher-Librarian*
- *Voice of Youth Advocates (VOYA)*

Online Resources for Graphic Novel Reviews

- *School Library Journal*
     http://www.schoollibraryjournal.com/
- *Publisher's Weekly*
     http://www.publishersweekly.com/pw/home/index.html
- *No Flying, No Tights*
     http://www.noflyingnotights.com/index2.html
- *Cooperative Children's Book Center*
     http://www.education.wisc.edu/ccbc/
- *Booklist*
     http://www.booklistonline.com/
- *Bulletin of the Center for Children's Books*
     http://bccb.lis.illinois.edu/
- *The Horn Book*
     http://www.hbook.com/
- *Voice of Youth Advocates (VOYA)*
     http://www.voya.com/
- *ICv2*
     http://www.icv2.com/

Flip charts and white boards can be used for students to suggest graphic novel titles for the library, ensuring they have a role in collection development.

among the recipients. More information about the Harvey Award, including lists of previous winners, can be found at http://www.harveyawards .org/.

If there are other libraries nearby, or schools in your district with student populations similar to yours, looking through their online catalogs to learn what graphic novels they own can help you choose individual titles or series to purchase. Other facilities often have knowledgeable people on staff who are happy to talk about what is popular with their graphic novel readers (Serchay, 2008). Take advantage of this type of assistance to ensure you choose the best resources for your particular group of adolescents.

Don't forget to ask for advice from the most involved stakeholders—the patrons and students who will be reading the books. Be sure to consider their requests and recommendations. You would buy the latest hot fiction title if your readers were clamoring for it, wouldn't you? In some libraries, superhero graphic novels are most popular, while in others, patrons fight over who gets to read the latest volumes in their favorite manga series. Over time, you will gauge what to purchase through circulation data and reader requests, but it can be extremely helpful to discover from the start what your adolescent readers want.

A quick and easy way to collect recommendations is to create a bulletin or dry erase board with a prominent sign asking for suggestions about which graphic novels to purchase. Encourage patrons and students to jot down their ideas. To further involve adolescents who are already avid graphic novel readers, start a graphic novel advisory group to assist in making decisions about what books to order. Not only will this help you tremendously, it will give them a powerful voice and make them loyal library supporters and spokespeople. You, of course, will have the final say in selection, making certain the graphic novels are appropriate for your library or school.

The Bottom Line

Let your readers help select graphic novels—they will be thrilled you value their opinions.

Filling Curricular Needs

You now know how to select graphic novels for the reading needs of your adolescent students and patrons, but what about locating graphic novels for their curricular needs? If you already select materials for a school, you should have a thorough knowledge of your state's curriculum, along with an understanding of assignments and projects given by the teachers who are your colleagues. With the recent emphasis on content area nonfiction, it is becoming easier to locate quality nonfiction graphic novels that support school curriculum. The lists in this book will provide you with plenty of titles to consider, while Chapters 8 through 17 will show specific ways to use graphic novels in lessons—by adjusting lesson plans you may already use, or in ways you may never have considered.

Age and Developmental Appropriateness

When you select materials for a library or school that serves adolescents, you make judgment calls as to what is appropriate and which resources best suit their needs. Knowing their ages, developmental levels, reading abilities, and interests guide your decisions. Choosing appropriate fiction and nonfiction books for adolescents can be difficult at times, but choosing graphic novels is especially tricky because of the nature of images as opposed to text. Images are more accessible by browsers, and can more easily shock a reader or be taken out of context. Images stick with a person long after they are viewed. Care must be taken that the graphic novels you acquire are not too adult for the adolescents at your library or school.

It is not unusual for a graphic novel to seem appropriate at first, only to have one page—or even one panel—feature content or language too adult for your library or school population. The comic format is not only for children; just as there are text-only novels written for adults, many graphic novels are meant for adults, too. And graphic novels that may be fine for the adolescents in one specific library or school may not meet community standards for another. Graphic novels that are part of a series can "age up," as do some children's books—Harry Potter, for example. Early volumes in a graphic novel series may be tame, while subsequent volumes sometimes become edgier and contain more adult content (Serchay, 2008). All of these are reasons why it is a good idea to carefully examine graphic novels you are unsure of before purchasing them. You can then assess them based on the particular adolescents at your library or school.

Additional aids are available to determine suitability, including recommendations from the professional journals and jobbers mentioned above. Reviews in journals often give age- or grade-level suggestions, and you may already rely on these guidelines for other purchases. Furthermore, some comics and graphic novel publishers, and nearly all publishers of manga for children, include ratings on the covers of their books. There is no consistent universal rating system—and most are subjectively applied—but the ratings are helpful when determining which books are appropriate for various age groups. In 2007, manga publisher, Tokyopop developed a rating system that is used for each book it publishes with standards for the ratings developed under the direction of graphic novel expert Michele Gorman. Tokyopop examines content, evaluates it according to 40 different indicators, and then puts each book into one of the

Comics Ratings

Marvel Comics

- All Ages
- A (ages 9 and up)
- T+ (ages 13 and up)
- Parental Advisory (ages 15 and up)

Tokyopop

- All Ages
- Youth Age 10+
- Teen Age 13+
- Older Teen Age 16+
- Mature Ages 18+

VIZ Media

- All Ages
- Teen
- Teen Plus
- Mature

five age categories. Examples of rating systems of some of the larger publishers of comics can be found in the sidebar.

Be aware, however, that relying only on generic ratings, or recommendations created by others, can limit your adolescent patrons and students. Don't allow fear of controversy to keep you from selecting graphic novels you have previewed and feel comfortable with purchasing. If you err too much on the side of caution, you do a disservice to older adolescents. They may not be interested in reading books meant for younger readers and you may hear that dreaded phrase that there is "nothing good to read." Use the ratings as guidelines, but select the best age-appropriate graphic novels based on your own judgment and expertise.

Objections and Challenges

Any materials purchased for libraries or schools are open to complaints from concerned members of the community about content they might find objectionable. As mentioned before, graphic novels are susceptible to extra scrutiny because of the visual impact of their art and illustrations (Goldsmith, 2005; Miller, 2005; Serchay, 2008), and because of their very nature. There is that word "graphic," for one thing, which can mean "explicit," or even "pornographic" to those new to the format. Some people know nothing about graphic novels and are uninformed as to why they are in libraries and schools that serve children in the first place. Even some of your adolescent patrons or students may feel that way.

Not all graphic novels are meant to be read by children or adolescents, and even those that are—like books in any format—might contain subject matter that can offend some readers. Objectionable content found in graphic novels might include sexuality, nudity, violence, cultural or gender stereotypes, language, smoking, and drinking (Goldsmith, 2005). For example, superhero graphic novels might feature scantily clad women or scenes of bloody violence, or Japanese manga could contain scenes of characters bathing or peeping at someone dressing. An awareness of the possibility of potential problems, and related intellectual freedom issues, makes it all the more crucial that you consult your collection development and management policy as you add graphic novels to your library or school, and prepare yourself for questions that might arise. But, once again, there is good news—objections about graphic novels can be handled in the exact same manner as a challenge to any material. Careful selection, as well as educating your parents, patrons and students, can keep problems from occurring and minimize them if they do (Goldsmith, 2005).

What measures can you take to help deflect potential challenges? The first reaction from library or school staff is often the most critical; however, you might not be the person to first hear someone's complaint. It might be an office receptionist, a clerical library assistant, a school administrator, or a volunteer who happens to be shelving books. All those people should be instructed to send the complainant your way. Listening carefully to what the parent or patron is saying, and reacting calmly, is important. Remember, questions about materials in libraries and schools usually come from concerned parents. You want them to be involved in what their children are reading. Generally, they only want to have questions answered or to have their say, so a cordial, non-defensive conversation can go a long way toward defusing the situation. Now that you can cite graphic novel research, and explain how you provide reading materials for *all* adolescents, you will be less likely to face formal challenges.

If the person pursues the challenge, the American Library Association's site, "Banned and Challenged Books" (http://www.lita.org/ala/issuesadvocacy/banned/index.cfm), is your first line of defense, along with your local policy for reconsideration of materials. As with any book, if a graphic novel is reconsidered, it should be evaluated on its entirety—not just one section, one panel, or one word. Don't be afraid to reconsider its place in the collection just because it is a graphic novel. Treat it as you would any other resource.

Selection Criteria

Sometimes you may not be able to locate reviews of graphic novels you are considering purchasing or using in lessons. This is especially true of newer titles. Written reviews of graphic novels often lag behind what's available for text-only titles, and there are fewer reviews, overall, of graphic novels. Because of this, you will sometimes have to determine for yourself whether or not a graphic novel is a good choice for your library or school. The sidebar contains standardized, essential criteria to consider when evaluating graphic novels.

The criteria in this book were developed at a 2008 workshop, "Evaluation of Graphic Format Books," sponsored collaboratively by the Instructional Technology Division of the North Carolina Department of Instruction (NCDPI) and the North Carolina School Library Media Association (NCSLMA). The goal of the workshop was to develop criteria to evaluate graphic format resources. Participants at the workshop included NCDPI consultants, practicing school and academic librarians, and a library professor. The criteria provide guidelines to use when assessing a book's strengths and weaknesses. By using these standards when choosing graphic novels, you can be assured of always purchasing exemplary titles.

The Bottom Line

If you've followed your collection development policy, and used reviews and criteria to select the best graphic novels, you can confidently stand behind your choices.

Criteria to Evaluate Graphic Novels

For Fiction Graphic Novels

- **Text**
  - Writing style appropriate for intended audience in terms of reading level, word choice, sentence or non-traditional text structure, clarity, length, and interpretation
  - Use of traditional elements such as plot, setting, and characters is evident and skillful
  - Subject matter, concepts, and vocabulary relevant to students' ages, developmental levels, and abilities
  - Error-free and current information where required
  - Content compatible with the reader's intellectual maturity
  - Formatting (page layout, print size) reflects targeted students
  - Effective use of sections or chapter divisions
  - Narrative true to selected genre such as fantasy, short story, and "coming of age"
  - Relevant to state K-12 curriculum
- **Art**
  - **Cover**
    - Attractive
    - Clearly indicates topic/theme of book
    - Appropriate for targeted audience
  - **Interior Art**
    - Art and text are interdependent and aesthetically pleasing
    - Appropriate and relevant to graphic format and content
    - Use of a variety and appropriate symbolic art, such as text bubbles and graphical representations of sound effects and emotions
    - Adequate in size and legibility
    - Effective use of color and shading
    - Skillful use of sequential art, such as panels and gutters for transitions
- **Technical Qualities**
  - Appropriate paper size and quality
  - Effective page layout
  - Durability of binding

For Nonfiction Graphic Novels

- **Content**
  - **Accuracy**
    - Error-free and current information
    - Objective, balanced presentation of information
    - Bias-free viewpoints
    - Balanced representations of cultural, gender, ethnic, and racial groups

- **Appropriateness**
  - Writing style appropriate for intended audience in terms of reading level, word choice, sentence or non-traditional text structure, clarity, length, and interpretation
  - Content compatible with the reader's intellectual maturity
  - Subject matter, concepts, and vocabulary relevant to students' ages, developmental levels, and abilities
  - Formatting (page layout, print size) reflects targeted students
  - Relevant to state K-12 curriculum
- **Scope**
  - Sufficient information to cover the topic for the intended audience
  - Logical sequence of topics
  - Effective use of sections or chapter divisions

- **Art**
  - **Cover**
    - Attractive
    - Clearly indicates topic/theme of book
    - Appropriate for targeted audience
  - **Interior Art**
    - Art and text are interdependent and aesthetically pleasing
    - Appropriate and relevant to graphic format and content
    - Use of a variety and appropriate symbolic art, such as text bubbles and graphical representations of sound effects and emotions
    - Captions and labels when needed
    - Skillful use of sequential art, such as panels and gutters for transitions
    - Effective use of color and shading

- **Features**
  - **Table of Contents**
    - Accurate and exact
    - Annotated or use of subheadings
  - **Glossary**
    - Complete list of unfamiliar words and terms
    - Complete definitions
    - Pronunciation guide
  - **Documentation and Supplemental Resources**
    - References for additional information
    - Bibliography or webliography for research or "further reading" list
    - Suggestions for classroom activities or procedures
    - Instructional aids such as discussion questions, timelines, and writing prompts
  - **Index**
    - Accurate
    - Thorough

- **Technical Qualities**
  - Appropriate paper size and quality
  - Effective page layout
  - Durability of binding

References

Goldsmith, Francisca. *Graphic Novels Now: Building, Managing, and Marketing a Dynamic Collection.* Chicago, IL: American Library Association, 2005.

"Marvel Subscriptions." 2011. http://subscriptions.marvel.com/help/ (accessed February 23, 2011).

Miller, Stephen. *Developing and Promoting Graphic Novel Collections.* New York: Neal-Schuman Publishers, Inc., 2005.

"Our Ratings VIZ Media." 2011. http://ratings.viz.com (accessed February 23, 2011).

Serchay, David S. *Graphic Novels for Teens and Tweens.* New York: Neal-Schuman Publishers, Inc., 2008.

"Tokyopop Our Ratings." 2011. http://www.tokyopop.com/corporate/booksellers/879 (accessed February 23, 2011).

Print Graphic Novel Resources for Librarians and Teachers

- Bitz, M. *When Commas Meet Kryptonite: Classroom Lessons from the Comic Book Project.* New York: Teacher's College Press, Columbia University, 2010.
- Brenner, Robin. *Understanding Manga and Anime.* Westport, CT: Libraries Unlimited, 2007.
- Carter, J. Bucky. *Building Literacy Connections with Graphic Novels: Page by Page, Panel by Panel.* Urbana, IL: National Council of Teachers of English, 2007.
- Cary, S. *Going Graphic: Comics at Work in the Multilingual Classroom.* Portsmouth, NH: Heinemann, 2004.
- Cornog, Martha, and Timothy Perper. *Graphic Novels Beyond the Basics: Insights and Issues for Libraries.* Santa Barbara, CA: Libraries Unlimited, Imprint of ABC-CLIO, 2009.
- Frey, N., and Fisher D. *Teaching Visual Literacy: Using Comic Books, Graphic Novels, Anime, Cartoons, and More to Develop Comprehension and Thinking Skills.* Thousand Oaks, CA: Corwin Press, 2008.
- Gavigan, K. W., and M. Tomasevich. *Connecting Comics to Curriculum: Strategies for Grades 6–12.* Santa Barbara, CA: Libraries Unlimited, 2011.
- Goldsmith, Francisca. *Graphic Novels Now: Building, Managing, and Marketing a Dynamic Collection.* Chicago, IL: American Library Association, 2005.
- Goldsmith, Francisca. *Readers' Advisory Guide to Graphic Novels.* Chicago, IL: American Library Association, 2010.

- Gorman, Michele. *Getting Graphic! Using Graphic Novels to Promote Literacy with Pre-Teens and Teens.* Worthington, OH: Linworth Publishing, Inc., 2003.
- Kan, Kat. *Graphic Novels and Comic Books: The Reference Shelf.* New York: H. W. Wilson Company, 2010.
- Miller, Stephen. *Developing and Promoting Graphic Novel Collections.* New York: Neal- Schuman Publishers, Inc., 2005.
- Monnin, Katie. *Teaching Graphic Novels: Practical Strategies for the Secondary ELA Classroom.* Gainesville, FL: Maupin House, 2010.
- Rourke, James. *The Comic Book Curriculum: Using Comics to Enhance Learning and Life.* Santa Barbara, CA: Libraries Unlimited, 2010.
- Weiner, Robert G. *Graphic Novels and Comics in Libraries and Archives: Essays on Readers, Research, History and Cataloging.* Jefferson, NC: McFarland & Co., 2010.

Online Graphic Novel Resources for Librarians and Teachers

Comics in Education
    http://www.humblecomics.com/comicsedu/index.html

Comics in the Classroom
    http://comicsintheclassroom.net/index.htm

Graphic Classroom
    http://graphicclassroom.blogspot.com

Graphic Novel Resources
    http://graphicnovelresources.blogspot.com

Graphic Novel Resources for Teachers and Librarians—University of Buffalo Library
    http://library.buffalo.edu/libraries/asl/guides/graphicnovels

Great Graphic Novels for Teens—YALSA
    http://www.ala.org/ala/yalsa/booklistsawards/greatgraphicnovelsforteens/gn.htm

Librarian's Guide to Anime and Manga
    http://www.koyagi.com/Libguide.html

My Comic Shop—Lists publishers' websites
    http://www.mycomicshop.com/graphicnovels

No Flying! No Tights!
    http://www.noflyingnotights.com/index2.html

*The listserv, Graphic Novels in Libraries, is another valuable resource for librarians. http://groups.yahoo.com/group/GNLIB-L
    †Several book jobbers/vendors also have helpful information on their websites.
    ‡Your local comic book shop is a great place to go for recommendations.

Chapter 3

Here You Come to Save the Day: Building Your Graphic Novel Collection

With the help of the selection guidelines and title lists in this book, along with some professional reviews and student recommendations, you now know which graphic novels to purchase. You can take a deep breath—the most time-consuming part is finished, and it gets easier from this point. There are other questions to ponder, though. How will you pay for the graphic novels? Where should you buy them? How do you get them ready for your patrons or students to use? This chapter will help you through each of these steps.

Budget Considerations

Because they have an obligation to spend their shrinking budgets wisely, librarians and teachers have to make tough decisions when buying books. Purchases should support the state curriculum, foster literacy, and nurture lifelong readers. Back when comics and graphic novels were a relatively new phenomena for schools and libraries, many people were skeptical about using taxpayer-supplied funds to buy them. Prior to 2002, it was a brave librarian or teacher who spent available money on comics, other than the occasional series title, such as *Peanuts* (Schultz), *Garfield* (Davis), or *Calvin and Hobbes* (Watterson). Far-seeing folks who wanted to give the graphic novel format a try often came up with alternate sources of funding to cautiously begin a collection. These sources are still available for the faint hearted or those with limited budgets, and include book fair funds, grants, and gifts from parent-teacher associations.

Library organizations, corporations and businesses, and education associations regularly give out grants. Someone has to win them, so why shouldn't it be you? Organizations that award grants are open to new ideas about using alternative formats to get adolescents interested in reading, and graphic novels are a terrific choice for an innovative program. Linking the program directly to curriculum and student achievement—as this book will enable you to do—will make your grant idea a frontrunner for winning. Parents are a great source for grants, too. Often, their workplaces offer grants

The Bottom Line

Buying graphic novels is money well-spent, with immediate rewards in terms of readership and excitement.

or matching funds for employees' local schools, and parents are thrilled to help their children's schools in this way.

Don't underestimate the power of your PTA or PTO to provide money for programs they feel will benefit students at your school. An active PTA raises money each year to spend directly on school programs and to help teachers provide resources for classrooms. Talk to your PTA president or staff liaison about your ideas to add more graphic novels to your school. Now that you are an expert on the benefits of using graphic novels in schools, you can enthusiastically describe what you want to do, along with the ways it will positively impact students.

The days when librarians and teachers became nervous when thinking about using library or school funding toward the purchase of graphic novels should be past. Today, the lines between text-only books and graphic novels have blurred. Young Adult novels include many more illustrations than before, and some, like Jeff Kinney's *Diary of a Wimpy Kid* series, include chunks of sequential art. Graphic novels have won prestigious children's book awards and are considered "literature" in the same way as text-only books. Don't push graphic novels to some secondary list—that "If Only I Had Enough Money" wish list. Graphic novels have gone mainstream, and they deserve a portion of your budget money as much as other types of books you buy to support instruction, or for adolescents' reading enjoyment.

Few teachers will invest in a large number of graphic novels for a classroom library. They are expensive, they go missing easily, and they wear out relatively quickly because they are handled so much. In the majority of schools, most graphic novels are purchased for the school library and reside there for all staff and students to use. Once you find individual titles that work seamlessly within your curriculum and lessons, you can buy your own copies to keep and use, because it's likely that whenever you want to use a specific graphic novel it will be checked out already and in the hands of another reader.

How many graphic novels should you buy when starting a collection for a school library? Budget dollars in libraries and schools are stretched thinner than ever, yet buying only a few graphic novels won't have the impact with students that a larger number will. Start as small as you have to; but remember, part of the justification for buying graphic novels for a library is to get students reading, facilitating an increase in circulation, and maintaining enthusiasm. It's tough to do that with just a few books; however, with the right promotions it can be done. Still, if you can afford a bigger start, go for it.

For around $1,000 you can purchase approximately 100 paperback graphic novels—a beginning collection that will wow students and get them reading and talking. Appendix 1 and 2 (located on pages 151 and 155) are core lists of 100 titles recommended for middle and high school students. These selective lists offer a variety of titles, including superhero, manga, fiction, nonfiction, and adaptations. You can use these lists of suggested titles to help develop a balanced collection of graphic novel titles for your library.

Purchasing

You may not be able to purchase all the graphic novels you want from sources you usually use, and you might have to buy or order them from a number of different places. Though you have used the tools from Chapter 2 to pre-select graphic novels you are interested in, if you are not familiar first-hand with the books you are considering buying, a trip to a local bookstore or comic book store should be your first step. At this point, you should be armed with lists of recommended books and student requests. Putting a list together beforehand is important. Without one, you will feel like a student using Google for research—faced with too many choices and overwhelmed by sheer numbers.

Visiting a bookstore or comic book store accomplishes two things. First, you can handle the graphic novels, read through some of them, preview several different series, and see the ratings on many of the books. Second, these stores usually have extremely helpful employees who love to talk about comics. Their help is invaluable when looking for popular graphic novels that adolescents will actually want to read. They know what teens are buying, what books are acclaimed, what graphic novels are being made into movies, and what will be published in the next few months. They might not know which graphic novels are appropriate for the adolescent population at your particular library or school, but by now you have criteria to help you make those decisions. And, you know your own readers better than anyone. You can decide what books are right for them. After a while, you will be able to flip through the pages of a graphic novel in a couple of minutes and tell at a glance whether it is suitable. If you do buy locally, and you work in a school, ask if they offer an educational discount. Many stores do.

Book jobbers and vendors you probably already use offer thousands of graphic novels, along with handy lists of award-winning or recommended titles. Once you have previewed and chosen which graphic novels to buy, books can be ordered from jobbers with cataloging records and processing included, if desired. Vendors and jobbers are especially good at stocking older volumes of graphic novels that stores no longer carry, if some of yours have gone lost or missing. But the best thing about book jobbers is the additional choice of bindings that are usually available.

Historically, graphic novels have sometimes been printed on inferior paper with weak glue and flimsy bindings (Goldsmith, 2005; Miller, 2005). Glossy pages in superhero books were especially problematic—after just a few checkouts, nearly every page in some comics would begin to come loose. The quality of bindings has improved; but because most graphic novels are published in paperback, they last only so long. Book jobbers often offer several choices of bindings. By all means, order stronger bindings if you can, but be aware that a jobber-bound book is usually twice the cost of the paperback version. You will have to choose whether quality or quantity is more important. It may be a good idea to start with a majority of paperbacks until you determine what is going to be most popular in your library or school. Once a paperback wears out and needs to be replaced, a stronger binding is an excellent choice and worth the additional expense.

Collection Management

Once the graphic novels are purchased, keeping track of them is essential to make sure patrons or students return them. If you are a classroom teacher, you will need to come up with a lending system to monitor student checkout, and, if you are a librarian, the new books will need to be cataloged, processed, and shelved. Each library, depending on its physical layout and logistics, will handle these things in slightly different ways. The most important factor is easy access, by both browsers and avid graphic novel readers. Patrons and students need to be able to quickly and conveniently locate what they are looking for.

It is also a tremendously important factor to have the ability to track the use of your graphic novels. In these assessment-driven times, data collection has become a vital element of what all librarians must do to justify their services, and school librarians have to show the impact of their library programs on student achievement. This can be nebulous and difficult to do. Research shows that adolescents who read more are better readers (Krashen, 2004), so book checkout is one piece of data that is not only valuable, but can easily be collected and analyzed via today's sophisticated circulation software. By tracking circulation, you can see how often graphic novels are checked out, and which patrons or students are reading them. You can calculate what percent of circulation is due to graphic novels, versus the percent of the collection made up of graphic novels. It's an excellent way to justify the addition of graphic novels to your library or school collection, as well as answer naysayers who may question their purchase and use. As mentioned in Chapter 1, as your graphic novels soar off the shelves, you will be amazed at the increase in circulation.

Cataloging and Shelving

How your graphic novels are cataloged and where they are shelved can have a large influence on how frequently they are used. Questions about cataloging and shelving can go on for days (and has, on some library listservs). Ask twenty librarians how they handle these issues and you are likely to get twenty different answers. Making thoughtful decisions about cataloging and shelving now will help immensely in avoiding problems in the future, so take some time to determine what will work best for your collection. In the sidebar are some questions to consider before you start.

Most libraries catalog and organize graphic novels in one of the following ways, and these

- Where is the 741.5 section of the library located? Is it easily accessible to students dashing in to grab a graphic novel or two? Is there ample room to add dozens—or hundreds—of books?
- Is there space in the library to place separate freestanding shelving that will accommodate all the graphic novels? Can the area be easily monitored by staff? Is it close enough to the circulation desk so books can be reshelved without too much effort?
- If you place all graphic novels—fiction and nonfiction—together, how will you make sure students and teachers find those related to their interests and curricular needs?

are the organizational methods most recommended (Goldsmith, 2005; Lyga, 2004; Miller, 2005):

- Use the Dewey classification 741.5 for all graphic novels, both fiction and non-fiction, and shelve them there—or in a separate, prime location, if space allows.
- Create a separate collection for graphic novels, or give them a GN prefix. Keep all graphic novels—fiction and nonfiction—together. Give fiction graphic novels a call number that includes the GN prefix, a fiction designation, and a cutter. Nonfiction graphic novels are given the GN prefix, the Dewey number for the topic of the book, and a cutter. Shelve them together in a separate, prime location.
- A combination of these approaches, depending on your facility's layout.

Though each method has advantages, they have disadvantages, as well. Graphic novels should be easily located by both browsers and searchers, but a 741.5 call number can be confusing. Nonfiction graphic novels will be overlooked by students doing research if those books have a GN or 741.5 call number. Fans of authors like Shannon Hale or Neil Gaiman will miss those author's graphic novels if they are shelved apart from their fiction work. Students who are intimidated by graphic novels and their unique format will not happen upon one if graphic novels are kept apart from everything else (Miller, 2005). You must weigh all these factors, consider your own circumstances, and make decisions that will be in the best interests of those using the books.

Assigning graphic novels a 741.5 or GN designation will allow you to easily look at a shelf list of all graphic novel titles and track their circulation. If nonfiction graphic novels have a 741.5 call number, be sure to give them subject headings that reflect their topics. Give all graphic novels a "Graphic Novels" subject heading. Not only will it help patrons using the library catalog, it will also enable you to analyze your library's data according to those terms.

Shelving

Have you ever planted a shrub, only to have it outgrow its spot because you underestimated the amount of space it would eventually need? A similar thing can happen with graphic novels, and once you own all 20-some volumes of a popular manga series you might find yourself scratching your head, wondering where to put them all. However, if you spread your books out too much, the shelves will appear empty once the books circulate regularly. By using freestanding shelves you can avoid problems and allow space for the growth of the collection. Mobile shelves offer the additional advantage of moving the collection from time to time, keeping things fresh and interesting.

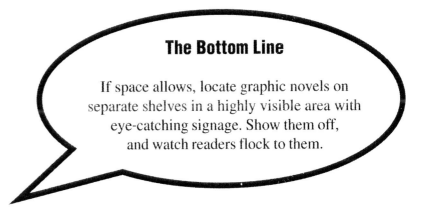

The Bottom Line

If space allows, locate graphic novels on separate shelves in a highly visible area with eye-catching signage. Show them off, and watch readers flock to them.

A Few Words about Processing

- Paperback graphic novels hold up much better if covered with book jackets or clear adhesive paper.
- Colorful graphic novel labels on the spines of books help patrons find them quickly and make shelving easier.
- Be careful not to cover volume numbers with spine labels.
- Manga books are tricky to process. The books read from back to front, so be sure to adjust your ownership markings accordingly.

Bookstores use many clever marketing techniques, and you can utilize some with your graphic novel collection. Covers of graphic novels contain fabulous artwork that deserves to be seen. Shelving as many graphic novels as possible face out is a great way to attract attention and make them accessible to adolescents (Miller, 2005; Goldsmith, 2005). The shelves will tend to be messy and should be straightened regularly. A quick trip to the shelves a couple of times a day to shelve and straighten will keep them looking good.

Promotion

If you've followed some of the guidelines in this book, your graphic novels will promote themselves, with little effort required. But if you slightly alter the promotions you probably already do, you can ensure even more attention from students and patrons.

First, if you discourage or do not allow books to be reserved or held in the library, consider changing that policy. Keeping up with reserves takes time and effort, and if you are the sole librarian it may be difficult to manage certain circulation tasks. But many graphic novel series contain volumes ending with cliffhangers that are meant to be read in order and, because of their popularity, desired volumes may be checked out. If adolescents aren't able to get the volumes they crave, they may become frustrated

Quick and Easy Promotion Ideas

- Be sure to have conspicuous, attractive signage for the collection.
- When you create book displays around themes or subjects, incorporate a few graphic novels.
- If you do book talks, include graphic novels. Be sure to show some of the art to your audience.
- If your library or school maintains literature lists—lists of suggested or required reading—add graphic novel titles to it.
- Make your graphic novel shelves more inviting by creating a striking display of pages of sequential art. Use pages from worn-out books that are to be discarded. Cut out colorful pages, mount them on cardstock, and laminate them.
- If the graphic novels aren't attracting browsers, they may be hidden. Move them to a more obvious, easy-to-access location.
- Adolescents love sharing their opinions. Survey them regularly to find out which graphic novels they like best, and what other titles or series they would like to read.

and give up. The amount of additional administrative effort required by allowing students to reserve what they want is easily offset by the rewards of getting books into readers' hands. Graphic novels go out and come back so rapidly that students usually don't have to wait too long to continue reading a series they are eager to finish. If fact, you will get to know your graphic novel readers and their tastes very well. You'll see them every day—possibly several times a day. They will become your best customers.

As mentioned in Chapter 1, some staff members, parents, or teachers might not be sold on the idea of graphic novels in libraries or classrooms, but what about adolescents who have never read one? A little lesson about graphic novels and their sequential art goes a long way toward convincing all readers to give them a try. Some lesson ideas are given later in this book. Suggestions for more formal programs to create excitement about graphic novels can be found in the sidebar, with graphic novel activities to try with your patrons and students.

Graphic novels will jump off your library shelves when you use displays like this.

Maintaining

Keeping graphic novels in good condition takes regular maintenance. Like paperback books and magazines, graphic novels become worn after they circulate many times. They require continual repair, usually because of loose pages or worn covers. When pages fall out of unpaged books, it can be especially challenging to put them back in order. Adolescents occasionally give in to temptation and tear out favorite

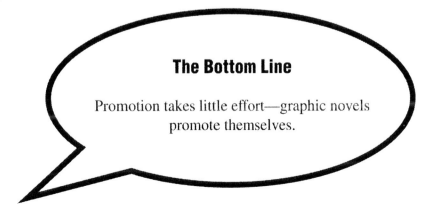

The Bottom Line

Promotion takes little effort—graphic novels promote themselves.

Programming with Graphic Novels: Quick and Easy Ideas

- Participate in Diamond Comics' "Free Comic Book Day" http://www.freecomicbookday.com
- Begin a Comics Club, a Manga Club, or an Anime Club
- Start a Book Club that reads and discusses graphic novel titles
- Have an anime screening party
- Hold cartooning workshops
- Host an Author/Artist visit
- Host a bookstore or comic book store visit by a graphic novel expert
- Oversee a manga book swap
- Have a "cosplay"—or costume play—party, with adolescents dressed as their favorite graphic novel characters
- Hold sessions about Japanese culture—the language, writing, tea ceremony, dress, origami, sushi
- Have a Comic Drawing Contest
- Have readers create their own manga characters or their own superheroes

pages. Volumes in a series get lost. You probably won't have to weed your graphic novel collection of items that don't circulate, but it's important to remove books that become too worn. If a graphic novel gets to that point it is because it is well read, and it deserves to be replaced (Miller, 2005). If it is part of a series, you will want to replace lost or worn volumes so readers can enjoy the entire series.

Once you start a graphic novel collection, there are compelling reasons to add to it. After some period of time, circulation of graphic novels will slow down, as patrons read their way through the collection. When you add additional volumes and new titles, circulation will jump again. Adolescents will check them out, devour them, and return them quickly to get more.

References

Goldsmith, Francisca. *Graphic Novels Now: Building, Managing, and Marketing a Dynamic Collection*. Chicago, IL: American Library Association, 2005.

Krashen, Stephen. *The Power of Reading*. Englewood, CO: Libraries Unlimited, 1993.

Lyga, Allyson A. W., and Barry Lyga. *Graphic Novels in Your Media Center: A Definitive Guide*. Westport, CT: Libraries Unlimited, 2004.

Miller, Stephen. *Developing and Promoting Graphic Novel Collections*. New York: Neal-Schuman Publishers, Inc., 2005.

The Bottom Line

Care for your graphic novels the way you do your garden—maintain it regularly and give it room to grow.

Chapter 4

Introducing Graphic Novels to Your Colleagues and Students

Hopefully, you are feeling like a graphic novel guru by now. You are armed with research, criteria, review sources, and more to help you develop quality graphic novel collections. Your excitement may wane, however, when you realize that some of your fellow librarians and teachers do not know the first thing about graphic novels, much less using them with patrons and students.

Fortunately, there are some hands-on activities you can use to help your colleagues become familiar with a variety of graphic novel titles. These activities are also designed to help librarians and educators share their ideas for using graphic novels with students and patrons. You can also use these activities with middle and high school students to introduce them to graphic novels in your collections.

The following five activities can be used as part of a professional development session on graphic novels held during a faculty meeting, library meeting, or conference. Depending on the amount of time you have available, you can use one or all of the activities as part of your training session.

Genre Sort

Purpose: This activity introduces participants to graphic novels in a variety of genres. It also provides participants with the opportunity to break into small groups to develop graphic novel activities to use in their libraries and classrooms.

Materials needed:

- One table for each group of participants (5–10 participants per group)
- On each table, place several graphic novels that represent a variety of genres.
- Provide each group with a flip chart and markers.

Introduction: Graphic novels represent many different genres. All genres such as biography, science fiction, historical non-fiction, fantasy, and so on are possible subjects for graphic novels. For this activity, you will examine the books with other members in your group and determine which genre is represented by each title you examine. You will also come up with a list of ideas for using graphic novels with students.

Preparation: Break the participants into small groups (5–10 participants per group).

Directions:

- Once you are at the table with your respective groups, elect a leader to facilitate discussion, as well as a scribe to take notes on the flip chart paper.
- Next, you and your colleagues will examine the various graphic novels provided at your table. Pass the titles around so that everyone has a chance to examine them. With others in your group, share your thoughts about how you would classify each book by genre.
- Discuss within your group the justification for your decisions. Talk about whether or not you were surprised by the variety of genres available in the graphic novel format.
- With the other members in the group, develop some ideas for activities that you could use with these genre titles in your libraries and classrooms.
- Post your suggested activities on a piece of chart paper that is provided on the table.
- Hang your group's completed chart on the wall.
- Once all groups have posted their charts, everyone will view the ideas on the charts via a walk-around "Museum Tour."

Adaptations Activity

Purpose: This activity introduces participants to graphic novel renditions of original works of literature and provides participants with the opportunity to break into small groups to develop activities for use in their libraries and classrooms.

Materials needed:

- One table for each group of participants (5–10 participants per group)
- On each table, place at least one example of a classic adaptation title for each participant in the group.
- Provide each group with a flip chart and markers.

Introduction: Literary works on all levels are now being adapted into the graphic novel format:

- Folk and fairy tales, e.g., *Jack and the Beanstalk* and *Paul Bunyan*
- Popular novels, e.g., *Artemis Fowl* and *Maximum Ride*
- Traditional classics, e.g., *Romeo and Juliet* and *Beowulf*

In this activity, you will examine graphic novel titles that are adaptations of other works of literature.

Preparation: Break the participants into small groups (5–10 participants per group).

Directions:

- Once you are at the table with your respective groups, elect a leader to facilitate discussion, as well as a scribe to take notes on the flip chart paper.

- Next, you and your colleagues will examine the titles provided at your table. Pass the titles around so that everyone has a chance to examine them. You will then discuss ideas for using these titles in your libraries and classrooms.

- Be sure to brainstorm curriculum-related activities. Consider various skill levels and special needs, such as academically gifted, English as a Second Language (ESL), lower-level, and reluctant readers.

- Post your suggested activities on a piece of chart paper that is provided on the table.

- Hang your group's completed chart on the wall.

- Once all groups have posted their charts, everyone will view the ideas on the charts via a walk-around "Museum Tour."

Biography Bash

Purpose: This activity introduces participants to graphic novel biographies and provides participants with the opportunity to break into small groups to develop activities to use in their libraries and classrooms.

Materials needed:

- One table for each group of participants (5–10 participants per group)

- On each table, place at least one example of a graphic novel biography for each participant in the group.

- Provide each group with a flip chart and markers.

Introduction: Biographies in a graphic novel format can deepen understanding when students use illustrations to facilitate their comprehension about a person and the time period in which he or she lived.

In this activity, you will examine graphic novel biographies with others in your group and plan activities for using them in your libraries and classrooms.

Preparation: Break the participants into small groups (5–10 participants per group).

Directions:

- Once you are at the table with your respective groups, elect a leader to facilitate discussion, as well as a scribe to take notes on the flip chart paper.

- Next, you and your colleagues will examine the titles provided at your table. Pass the titles around so that everyone has a chance to examine them. You will then discuss ideas for using these biographies in your libraries and classrooms

- Be sure to brainstorm curriculum-related activities. Consider various skill levels and special needs, such as academically gifted, English as a Second Language (ESL), lower-level, and reluctant readers.

- Post your suggested activities on a piece of chart paper that is provided on the title.

- Hang your group's completed chart on the wall.
- Once all groups have posted their charts, everyone will view the ideas on the charts via a walk-around "Museum Tour."

Let's Get "Series-ous" about Graphic Novels!

Purpose: This activity introduces participants to titles in graphic novel series. It also provides participants with the opportunity to break into small groups to develop activities to use in their libraries and classrooms.

Materials needed:

- One table for each group of participants (5–10 participants per group).
- On each table, place several examples of graphic novel series titles for each participant in the group.
- Provide each group with a flip chart and markers.

Introduction: Series books provide extra support to readers because of the consistencies from one book to another. They enable readers to become familiar with the ways that authors present setting, characters, and plot. There are numerous graphic novel series available for K-12 students.

In this activity, you will examine graphic novel titles that are in a series and discuss ways to use them in your libraries and classrooms.

Preparation: Break the participants into small groups (5–10 participants per group).

Directions:

- Once you are at the table with your respective groups, elect a leader to facilitate discussion, as well as a scribe to take notes on the flip chart paper.
- Next, you and your colleagues will examine the series titles provided at your table. Pass the titles around so that everyone has a chance to examine the fiction and non-fiction graphic novel series in your group.
- With your group, brainstorm ways in which you can use these titles across the curriculum. Consider various skill levels and special needs, such as academically gifted, English as a Second Language (ESL), lower-level, and reluctant readers.
- Post your suggested activities on a piece of chart paper that is provided at your table.
- Hang your group's completed chart on the wall.
- Once all groups have posted their charts, everyone will view the ideas on the charts via a walk-around "Museum Tour."

Manga Activity

Purpose: This activity introduces participants to manga titles. It also provides participants with the opportunity to break into small groups to discuss the characteristics of manga and the ways they can be used in their libraries and classrooms.

Materials needed:

- One table for each group of partici- pants (5–10 partici- pants per group)
- On each table, place at least one manga title for each partici- pant in the group.
- Provide each group with a flip chart and markers.

Series books are important staples in graphic novel and manga col- lections.

Introduction: Manga (pro- nounced Mahn-gah) is a unique Japanese style of graphic novels that reads from back to front, and right to left. Many manga titles are illustrated in black and white, and they use an exaggerated Japanese style to represent characters in the series. Manga titles are often gender-specific. For example, *shônen* comics are written for males, from ages twelve to eighteen years, while *shôjo* is written for females. For this activity, you will examine manga titles and discuss their charac- teristics with other members in your group.

Preparation: Break the participants into small groups (5–10 participants per group).

Directions:

- Once you are at the table with your respective groups, elect a leader to facilitate discussion, as well as a scribe to take notes on the flip chart paper.
- Next, you and your colleagues will examine the various manga titles pro- vided at your table. Pass the titles around so that everyone has a chance to examine them.
- With others in your group, share your thoughts about the characteristics of manga. Discuss the ways in which they differ from other graphic novels.
- Share your ideas on why you think manga is so popular with middle and high school readers. Post these ideas on a piece of chart paper that is pro- vided on the table.
- Hang your group's completed chart on the wall.
- Once all groups have posted their charts, everyone will view the ideas on the charts via a walk-around "Museum Tour."

Additional information about manga can be found in the following chapter, Manga 101.

Chapter 5

Manga 101

In the world of graphic novels, manga can be particularly perplexing, even to those familiar with the comic format. This chapter will explain the basics of manga and its tremendous popularity. Even if you don't become an avid manga reader, you will be able to appreciate it and better understand its appeal to children and adolescents.

Simply put, manga are Japanese comics. Contemporary manga developed in Japan after World War II. Manga gradually found its way to the United States and by the mid-1990s its popularity had grown tremendously, helped along by Japanese video games and anime—animated versions of Japanese comics (Brenner, 2007). Beginning around 2001, manga captured an ever-increasing segment of the growing graphic novel market (Thompson, 2007) and still accounts for a large portion of graphic novels published in America (ICV2, 2010).

Because most manga is Japanese, it is generally printed in a direction Westerners consider back to front and right to left. Thus, the story starts at what you may consider the back of the book. For those who are unfamiliar with the format, the process of reading manga can be a challenge. Manga titles published in the United States often come with prompts at the beginning and end of the book to help guide readers. The method of reading manga isn't the only thing that's different, however. Characters, elements, and story lines are unlike those in other types of graphic novels and take some getting used to.

The art in manga has a unique look. It is usually printed in black and white and, although it is sequential art, the panels often flow into one another, with fewer gutters and with panels of mixed sizes. Characters are slim, with long legs and large eyes, and males and females have a similar, androgynous look. Manga titles contain many sound effects and a great deal of emotion, shown with exaggerated expressions. Whereas children's books in America sometimes include potty humor and jokes about underwear, manga books may contain gender-role mix-ups, sexual tension, risqué humor, and occasional nudity. Cultural differences account for the disparity. Manga are Japanese comics and they reflect the humor, formulas, and style that are popular there.

So, why are some American adolescents so obsessed with manga? Is it the lively story lines, the angst, the beautiful characters with impossibly luxurious hair, the embarrassing situations, the romance? It may be all of these; however, in anecdotal interviews and discussions with younger adolescents, many indicated they liked manga for the fast-paced, fun, action-filled stories. Often, they watched anime versions

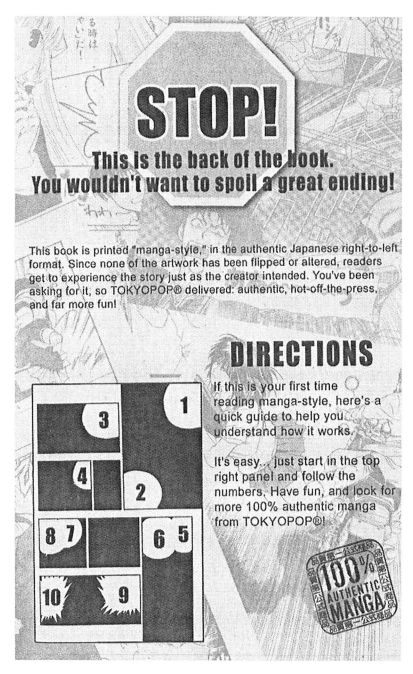

© TOKYOPOP, Inc.

of the stories first and then found the manga. See the sidebar on pages 39-40 for some fascinating, detailed comments made by older adolescents in an anonymous online book discussion group, when asked why they like manga.

Because there is often similarity between the artwork in manga titles, it may be difficult to distinguish between them. However, manga features the same genres and subjects you find in other books: fantasy, science fiction, realistic, historical, sports, romance, mystery, and nonfiction. Also, it is written for different age groups—including adults. Manga titles are anything but simple; in fact, most are multifaceted and complex. They require readers to interpret not only the plot and the detailed art, but also occasional Chinese text and Asian culture, all while reading in a direction that's new to them (Schwartz and Rubenstein-Ávila, 2006). Though there are stand-alone titles, manga storylines are often published in multiple volumes, and it is not unusual to find 20 or 30 volumes in a series. The storylines often leave the reader hanging, so adolescents will clamor for those additional volumes of their favorite series.

Anyone hesitant about adding manga to a school or library should read Robin Brenner's excellent book, *Understanding Manga and Anime* (Libraries Unlimited, 2007), to get a more detailed explanation and deeper appreciation of Japanese comics. Brenner's book covers all aspects of manga and anime, including the reasons they are so remarkably popular with children and adolescents. Next, read some manga yourself to get a feel for the style. You might discover what your students and patrons find so satisfying in these books and get hooked on the characters, their exploits, the emotion, and the plot twists.

References

"A Second Bad Year in a Row for Manga." ICV2. Apr 16, 2010. http://www.icv2.com/articles/index_print.php?article_id=17292 (accessed July 12, 2010).

Brenner, Robin E. *Understanding Manga and Anime*. Westport, CT: Libraries Unlimited, 2007.

Schwartz, Adam, and Eliane Rubinstein-Ávila. "Understanding the manga hype: Uncovering the multimodality of comic-book literacies." Journal of Adolescent & Adult Literacy 50, no. 1 (September 1, 2006): 40–49. http://www.proquest.com/ (accessed January 24, 2011).

Thompson, Jason. "How Manga Conquered the US." *Wired*. Nov. 2007.

The Vocabulary of Manga

Manga: Japanese comics.

Anime: A shortened Japanese pronunciation of animation.

Shônen: Manga for males 12 to 18. Story lines often include action, adventure, and humor.

Shôjo: Manga for females. Story lines often include relationships and romance.

Manhua: Manga from Taiwan.

Manhwa: Manga from South Korea.

OEL Manga: Original English Language manga.

Manga Otaku: An obsessed fan of Japanese manga.

Suggested Titles for Middle and High Schools (MS & HS)

Kouno, Fumiyo. *Town of Evening Calm: Country of Cherry Blossoms*. San Francisco, CA: Last Gasp, 2007. (HS)

Takada, Rie, Lance Caselman, and Noritaka Minami. *Gaba Kawa*. San Francisco, CA: Viz Media, 2008. (MS & HS)

Tatsumi, Yoshihiro, Adrian Tomine, Taro Nettleton, and Yoshihiro Tatsumi. *A Drifting Life*. Montreal: Drawn & Quarterly, 2009. (HS)

Suggested Titles in a Series

*Arakawa, Hiromu. *Fullmetal Alchemist* Series. San Francisco, CA: Viz Media. (MS & HS)

Asada, Hiroyuki. *Tegami Bachi Letter Bee* Series. San Francisco, CA: Viz Media. (HS)

- I like manga primarily for the art, but even then I am picky. I used to like manga fairly indiscriminately, likely because it was so rare, but as more of it is brought over it seems that many of the stories are redundant in many aspects; some of the plots rely heavily on the same themes and clichés (giant robots, endless power-up battles, disproportionate magical schoolgirls—I can't stand shojo, manga for girls, because it is incredibly formulaic and sappy). Since it's a highly visual medium, not as much is left to the imagination . . . so I guess I think of it as fairly easy, fun reading. But if it hooks someone into reading (with segues such as the brand-new graphic novel of *Hamlet*, or Avi's *City of Light/City of Dark*, or even the Sandman series), then that's even better. It also promotes interest in Japanese culture and language, which is really cool. And the stories that ARE fresh and original are very well crafted, just as complex as any novel, and deal with fairly tough ethical themes ... it seems like the authors of manga really take a lot of pride in their stories.

- I read manga and other graphic novels for much the same reason that I read books—because I like the stories. Since I have a lot of interest in the visual arts as well, it's of interest to me to see how people integrate images and text to create a coherent work. If I don't like the story, I won't read it. What I like best about anime are the same things I like best about some books. An interesting, complex plot, characters who are interesting and fun to read about, and in the case of manga or graphic novels I like it when the art is at least decent.

- I read it for the plots (or sometimes the adorable lack thereof, in shojo manga) and the arts, and I only VERY rarely will read a manga in which I don't like the art style.

- I read manga for the same reasons I read novels I suppose. If it interests me, I'll read it. The artwork is the biggest draw for me. I tend to like stuff that's very detailed and stylized, and I'm also really drawn to the Manhwa style, which uses heavy lines. If the story sounds interesting, but I don't like the style of the art, I won't read it.

- In a way, they are a faster read. Though, if you sit down to read an entire series (several volumes), it's like reading a small novel. There's just a different way of processing them. When I read a book, I'm looking at the text on several levels. When I read a manga, there's the visual element to process as well.

- The biggest reason I read the manga is for the art (because some of it is pure gorgeous). If I read the manga for just the story line, I'd probably read it online, but because it's the art I love most, I hate to look at it on the computer screen where it's resized and doesn't always fit right on the screen.

Ashihara, Hinako. *Sand Chronicles* Series. San Francisco, CA: Viz Media. (HS)

*Azuma, Kiyohiko. *Yotsuba&!* Series. Houston, TX: ADV Manga. (MS)

Chmakova, Svetlana. *Dramacon* Series. Los Angeles, CA: Tokyopop. (HS)

Cibos, Lindsay. *Peach Fuzz* Series. Los Angeles, CA: Tokyopop Publishing. (MS)

CLAMP (Mangaka group). *Kobato* Series. New York: Yen Press. (HS)

*CLAMP (Mangaka group). *Tsubasa* Series. New York: Ballantine Books. (MS & HS)

Crilley, Mark. *Miki Falls* Series. New York: HarperTeen. (MS & HS)

Flanagan, William. *Fairy Tail* Series. New York: Ballantine Books. (MS & HS)

Ganter, Amy K. *Sorcerers & Secretaries* Series. Los Angeles, CA: Tokyopop Publishing.(MS & HS)

Higuchi, Daisuke. *Whistle!* Series. San Francisco, CA: VIZ Media. (MS)

Hikawa, Kyoko. *From Far Away* Series. San Francisco, CA: Viz Media. (MS & HS)

Himekawa, Akira. *The Legend of Zelda* Series. San Francisco, CA: Viz Media. (MS)

Hino, Matsuri. *Vampire Knight* Series. San Francisco, CA: Viz Media. (HS)

*Hotta, Yumi. *Hikaru No Go* Series. San Francisco, CA: Viz Media. (MS)

Igarashi, Daisuke. *Children of the Sea* Series. San Francisco, CA: Viz Media. (MS & HS)

Inada, Koji, and Shaenon K. Garrity. *Beet the Vandel Buster* Series. San Francisco, CA: VIZ Media. (MS)

Inagaki, Riichiro. *Eyeshield 21* Series. San Francisco, CA: VIZ Media. (HS)

Inoue, Takehiko. *Real* Series. San Francisco, CA: Viz Media. (HS)

Inoue, Takehiko. *Slam Dunk* Series. San Francisco, CA: Viz Media. (HS)

Itō, Junji. *Uzumaki* Series. San Francisco, CA: VIZ Media. (HS)

Iwahara, Yuji. *King of Thorn* Series. Los Angeles, CA: Tokyopop Publishing. (HS)

The Bottom Line

Many adolescent readers find manga original, interesting, and fun.

Iwaoka, Hisae. *Saturn Apartment* Series. San Francisco, CA: Viz Media. (MS & HS)

Izumi, Rei. *.hack// Legend of the Twilight* Series. Los Angeles, CA: Tokyopop Publishing. (MS)

Kanno, Aya. *Otomen* Series. San Francisco, CA: VIZ Media. (HS)

Kawahara, Kazune. *High School Debut* Series. San Francisco, CA: Viz Media. (MS & HS)

Kim, Tong-hwa. *The Color of Earth* Series. New York: First Second. (HS)

*Kishimoto, Masashi. *Naruto* Series. San Francisco, CA: Viz Media. (MS & HS)

Kobayashi, Miyuki. *Kitchen Princess* Series. New York: Ballantine Books. (MS & HS)

Koge, Donbo. *Pita-ten* Series. Los Angeles, CA: Tokyopop Publishing. (MS)

*Konomi, Takeshi. *The Prince of Tennis* Series. San Francisco, CA: Viz Media. (MS)

*Kubo, Tite. *Bleach* Series. San Francisco, CA: Viz Media. (MS & HS)

Kure, Yuki. *La Cordo d' Oro* Series. San Francisco, CA: Viz Media. (MS & HS)

Matsumoto, Nina. *Yōkaiden* Series. New York: Ballantine Books. (MS & HS)

*Miyazaki, Hayao. *Howl's Moving Castle* Series. San Francisco, CA: VIZ Media. (MS)

*Miyazaki, Hayao. *Nausicaa of the Valley of Wind* Series. San Francisco, CA: Viz Comics. (MS & HS)

*Miyazaki, Hayao. *Miyazaki's Spirited Away* Series. San Francisco, CA: Viz Communications. (MS)

Mori, Kaoru. *Emma* Series. La Jolla, CA: DC Comics. (HS)

Nakajo, Hisaya. *Sugar Princess* Series. San Francisco, CA: Viz Media. (MS)

*Oda, Eiichiro. *One Piece* Series. San Francisco, CA: Viz Media. (MS & HS)

Ohba, Tsugumi. *Death Note* Series. San Francisco, CA: VIZ Media. (HS)

Park, So Hee. *The Royal Palace Goong* Series. New York: Yen Press. (HS)

Patterson, James. *Maximum Ride* Series. New York: Yen Press. (MS)

*Ryukishi07. *Higurashi When They Cry* Series. New York: Yen Press. (HS)

Shan, Darren. *Cirque Du Freak* Series. New York: Yen Press. (MS & HS)

*Sugisaki, Yukiru. *D N Angel* Series. Los Angeles, CA: Tokyopop. (MS & HS)

*Takahashi, Rumiko. *Inu Yasha* Series. San Francisco, CA: Viz Media. (HS)

*Takahashi, Rumiko. *Ranma ½* Series. San Francisco, CA: Viz Media. (HS)

*Takaya, Natsuki. *Fruits Basket* Series. Los Angeles, CA: Tokyopop Publishing. (MS & HS)

Takei, Hiroyuki. *Shaman King* Series. San Francisco, CA: Viz Media. (MS & HS)

Toriyama, Akira. *Dragon Ball Z* Series. San Francisco, CA: Viz Comics. (MS)

Urasawa, Naoki. *Pluto Urasawa X Tezuka* Series. San Francisco, CA: Viz Media. (HS)

Watase, Yuu. *Arata, the Legend* Series. San Francisco, CA: Viz Media. (MS & HS)
*Watsuki, Nobuhiro. *Rurouni Kenshin* Series. San Francisco, CA: Viz Media. (HS)
Yaginuma, Kō. *Twin Spica* Series. New York: Vertical Press. (MS & HS)
*Yazawa, Ai. *Nana* Series. San Francisco, CA: VIZ Media. (HS)
Yoshizumi, Wataru. *Ultra Maniac* Series. San Francisco, CA: Viz Media. (MS)

---

*These titles are also produced in anime form.

Chapter 6

Superhero Graphic Novels: A Super Way to Lure Readers

If you are like most people, you read comic books as a child. You may have fond memories of lying on the floor next to a stack of comics that you read over and over. Your favorite comics may have featured Archie, Casper the Friendly Ghost, or Uncle Scrooge, but there were probably many comics in that stack that featured superhero characters. Since the 1930s, most Americans have grown up with superheroes like Batman, Superman, Spider-Man, Wonder Woman, and X-Men. Those unfamiliar with today's graphic novels may imagine them to be just like the superhero comics they read when they were young, and in some cases they would be correct. Though a wide variety of graphic novels are published each year, these same beloved superheroes are found within the pages of many today.

DC Comics introduced Superman to the world in 1938. Now a subsidiary of Warner Brothers and Time Warner, DC also created superheroes like Batman, Wonder Woman, and the Green Lantern (DC Comics, 2011). Marvel Comics, founded in 1939 and now owned by the Walt Disney Company, brought us characters like Spider-Man, X-Men, the Hulk, and Wolverine (Marvel Comics, 2011). Publishers of comics like DC, Marvel, Dark Horse, and Image have unveiled hundreds of superheroes over the decades. Some superhero characters have faded away, but others have remained as well-loved as ever.

Males of all ages are especially attracted to superhero comics, and this appeal, over the years, has not faded. Why are these comics still so popular? Some reasons relate to craftsmanship and marketing. Superhero comics have been written and illustrated by some of the best authors and artists in the business. Makers of superhero comics have enthusiastically changed with the times, with frequently revitalized storylines that include diverse characters and current issues, which keep them fresh and compelling. New readers have been attracted to the genre by related cartoons, television shows, video games, and movies. But an important reason that many readers, young and old, are loyal to superhero comic has to do with the conventions of the genre.

What is a hero? What qualities do most heroes share? Whether it is an ancient hero like Hercules or a fictional one like Superman, heroes in literature share common traits. They are courageous, talented, and resourceful. They are honorable, ethical, and altruistic, though sometimes out for revenge. They make their own rules. They are not

The Bottom Line

Superhero graphic novels—like the tales of ancient heroes—have an enduring appeal.

always born great, but are motivated by a fate or destiny they feel they must fulfill. They have a seemingly impossible task—a fight between good and evil. Superheroes have much in common with classical heroes, and their stories are timeless.

Superheroes have an additional allure, though. Most have extraordinary strengths, super powers, and cool technology. Superheroes often wear costumes to hide their true identities, adding an extra layer of mystique. Their enemies are usually super villains —megalomaniacs who want to destroy or take over the world. Superheroes are not without their weaknesses, though. Batman has no superpowers and can be harmed in many ways. Others, like Superman, have certain physical vulnerabilities—like exposure to Kryptonite—but the biggest challenge to them often involves rescuing people they love. Superhero graphic novels include many of the same elements as mythology and fantasy, and thus have a similar appeal. Readers can lose themselves in the superhero's world, escape from their own normal lives, and live vicariously through these powerful character's trials and triumphs.

An analysis of the motivations and characteristics of heroes—real, historical, and fictionalized—can make for interesting discussions with adolescents. The noble traits and strength of character often demonstrated by comic book superheroes can be used to help students understand ideals such as courage, selflessness and altruism (Rourke, 2010). Comparing and contrasting heroes can help students contemplate who they want to be, and how to be strong when temptation strikes or life gets hard. Superhero graphic novels can add an additional component to lessons that include more traditional heroes studied in middle and high school, like *The Illiad* and *The Odyssey*, or American tall tales.

Using superhero graphic novels with topics across the curriculum can also expand critical thinking and add an element of fun. For example, in their book, *Super-Powered Word Study*, Carter and Evensen (2010) use superheroes to teach words and word parts, and in *The Comic Book Curriculum*, Rourke (2010) ties lessons in history, civics, and literature into story lines from popular superhero comics. In addition, students can enjoy creating their own superheroes, through an online tool like the one at Marvel Comics' website *"Create Your Own Superhero"* (http://marvel.com/games/play/31/create_your_own_superhero) or through their own drawings. Students can choose the essential traits of their characters, select a name, design a costume, and create a place for them to live.

Superhero comics should also be an integral part of a graphic novel collection for pleasure reading. Adolescents who patronize your library or school media center will demand stories about superheroes. Like manga, if you are unfamiliar with the most popular, acclaimed titles, your patrons will be happy to help you choose the hottest series to purchase.

References

"About DC Comics." 2011. http://www.dccomics.com/dccomics/about/ (accessed January 25, 2011).

Carter, James Bucky, and Eric A. Evensen. *Super-powered Word Study: Teaching Words and Word Parts Through Comics*. Gainesville, FL: Maupin House, 2010.

"Marvel Comics." 2011. http://marvel.com/ (accessed January 25, 2011).

Rourke, James. *The Comic Book Curriculum: Using Comics to Enhance Learning and Life*. Santa Barbara, CA: Libraries Unlimited, 2010.

Suggested Titles for Middle and High Schools (MS & HS)

Busiek, Kurt. *Marvels*. New York: Marvel Publishing, 2008. (MS & HS)

Diggle, Andy, and Jock. *Green Arrow: Year One*. New York: DC Comics, 2008. (HS)

Dixon, Chuck, Scott Beatty, and Javier Pulido. *Robin: Year One*. New York: DC Comics, 2000. (MS & HS)

Giffen, Keith, and John Rogers. *Blue Beetle: Shellshocked*. New York: DC Comics, 2006. (MS & HS)

Giffen, Keith, and John Rogers. *Blue Beetle: Road Trip*. New York: DC Comics, 2007. (MS & HS)

Hine, David, Fabrice Sapolsky, and Giandomenico C. Di. *Spider-Man Noir: Eyes Without a Face*. New York: Marvel Pub, 2010. (MS & HS)

Johns, Geoff, Gary Frank, Jon Sibal, Rob Leigh, Steve Wands, and Brad Anderson. *Superman Brainiac*. New York: DC Comics, 2009. (MS & HS)

Johns, Geoff, and Ivan Reis. *Green Lantern: Secret Origin*. New York: DC Comics, 2008. (HS)

Kelly, Joe, and J. M. K. Niimura. *I Kill Giants*. Berkeley, CA: Image Comics, 2009. (HS)

Lethem, Jonathan, Karl Rusnak, and Farel Dalrymple. *Omega: The Unknown*. New York: Marvel, 2008. (HS)

Loeb, Jeph, and Tim Sale. *Superman for All Seasons*. New York: DC Comics, 1999. (MS & HS)

Loeb, Jeph, Tim Sale, and Bob Kane. *Batman: The Long Halloween*. New York: DC Comics, 1998. (MS & HS)

Miller, Frank. *Batman: The Dark Knight Returns*. New York: DC Comics. (HS)

Miller, Frank, and David Mazzucchelli. *Batman: Year One*. New York: DC Comics, 2005. (MS & HS)

Moore, Alan, Dave Gibbons, and John Higgins. *Watchmen*. New York: DC Comics, 2008. (HS)

Morrison, Grant. *Batman: The Return of Bruce Wayne*. New York: DC Comics, 2011. (HS)

Pak, Greg, Giandomenico C. Di, Matt Hollingsworth, Dave Lanphear, and Natalie Lanphear. *X-Men: Magneto Testament*. New York: Marvel Publishing, 2009. (HS)

Ross, Alex, Paul Dini, Jerry Siegel, and Joe Shuster. *Superman: Peace on Earth*. New York: DC Comics, 1999. (MS & HS)

Simone, Gail, and Aaron Lopresti. *Wonder Woman: Ends of the Earth*. New York: DC Comics, 2009. (MS & HS)

Simone, Gail, Terry Dodson, Bernard Chang, and Ron Randall. *Wonder Woman: the Circle*. New York: DC Comics, 2008. (MS & HS)

Smith, Jeff. *Shazam!: The Monster Society of Evil*. New York: DC Comics, 2007. (MS)

Straczynski, J. M., Shane Davis, and Sandra Hope. *Superman: Earth One*. New York: DC Comics, 2010. (HS)

Waid, Mark, and Leinil F. Yu. *Superman Birthright*. New York: DC Comics, 2004. (MS)

Suggested Titles in a Series

Batman: The Greatest Stories Ever Told Series. New York: DC Comics. (MS)

Brubaker, Ed, and Steve Epting. *The Death of Captain America* Series. New York: Marvel. (MS & HS)

Busiek, Kurt. *Astro City* Series. La Jolla, CA: Homage Comics. (MS & HS)

Card, Orson S. *Ultimate Iron Man* Series. New York: Marvel. (HS)

Grayson, Devin K., and Udon. *X-Men Evolution* Series. New York: Marvel. (MS)

The Immortal Iron Fist Series. New York: Marvel Publishing. (HS)

Jemas, Bill, Brian M. Bendis, and Mark Bagley. *Ultimate Spider-Man* Series. New York: Marvel Comics. (MS & HS)

Johns, Geoff, Dave Gibbons, and Peter Tomasi. *Green Lantern: The Sinestro Corps War* Series. New York: DC Comics. (HS)

Johns, Geoff. *Teen Titans* Series. New York: DC Comics. (MS)

Kirkman, Robert. *Invincible* Series. Berkeley, CA: Image Comics. (HS)

Loeb, Jeph, and Jim Lee. *Batman: Hush* Series. New York: DC Comics. (HS)

McKeever, Sean. *Sentinel* Series. Edina, MN: Spotlight. (MS)

Millar, Mark. *The Ultimate X-Men Collection* Series. New York: Marvel. (MS)

Morrison, Grant. *All-Star Superman* Series. New York: DC Comics. (MS & HS)

Rucka, Greg, and Ed Brubaker. *Gotham Central* Series. New York: DC Comics. (HS)

Spider-Man Visionaries Series. New York: Marvel Comics. (MS & HS)

Teitelbaum, Michael. *The Invincible Iron Man* Series. New York: DK Publishing. (MS & HS)

Vaughan, Brian K., and Tony Harris. *Ex Machina* Series. La Jolla, CA: WildStorm Productions/ DC Comics. (HS)

Vaughan, Brian K., and Adrian Alphona. *Runaways* Series. New York: Marvel Comics. (MS & HS)

Whedon, Joss, and John Cassaday. *Astonishing X-Men* Series. New York: Marvel Comics. (HS)

Chapter 7

Comics and Curriculum: Strategies and Lesson Plans

By now you should feel confident about including graphic novels in your library or school—justifying their addition, selecting and purchasing them, placing them in your library or classroom, and extolling their virtues from the rooftop. You may feel passionate about the role they can play in recreational reading and, if you have already purchased graphic novels, you may see that excitement reflected in your readers. Can you begin to envision their place within your school's curriculum?

If you are a school librarian or teacher, you support learning by differentiating the resources you utilize. You use short books and long ones, hard books and easy ones, different genres, videos and DVDs, audio books, e-books, articles, online resources, and more. Why not use graphic novels to support teaching and learning, too? Graphic novels can be a powerful tool to motivate learners of all abilities and backgrounds, and they can make tough topics—AIDS, Shakespeare, DNA, terrorism, cancer—more accessible to learners. If you have favorite lesson plans that effectively teach your curriculum, you can adapt those plans to include graphic novels. If you are a school librarian, you can collaborate with teachers to help them incorporate graphic novels into their instruction.

Chapters 8–18 provide excellent starting points, with ideas for using specific titles with subjects, objectives, and concepts that are widely taught in middle and high schools. Each chapter cites standards that the lessons support, with an appropriate AASL Standard for the 21st-Century Learner. These standards will enable you to justify the use of graphic novels in your libraries and classrooms. Next are *Comic Connections*, quick and easy ideas for integrating graphic novels into curricular areas. A list of recommended titles is at the end of each chapter, followed by a selective list of titles in a series.

Finally, a caveat. For as many avid adolescent graphic novel readers as there are, there are an equal number of students unfamiliar with them. Those adolescents may feel intimidated by the format, or carry stereotypes in their heads about what kind of reader is attracted to them. To understand the importance of visual literacy, and to appreciate graphic novels to the degree they deserve, students will first need an introduction to them.

Teaching Standards

Standards from the following national professional associations were considered in the preparation of this book. If you would like to access additional standards in preparing your lesson plans, please refer to the websites below.

- American Association of School Librarians (AASL)—Standards for the 21st-Century Learner (www.ala.org/ala/mgrps/divs/aasl/guidelinesandstandards/learningstandards/standards.cfm)
- Center for Civic Education—National Standards for Civics and Government (www.civiced.org/index.php?page=stds)
- Common Core State Standards Initiative—Common Core State Standards for English Language Arts and Mathematics (www.corestandards.org)
- National Standards for Arts Education (http://artsedge.kennedy-center.org/educators/standards.aspx)
- International Reading Association (IRA) and National Council of Teachers of English (NCTE)—Standards for the English Language Arts (compiled jointly by *NCTE* and *IRA* in 1996) (www.ncte.org/standards)
- National Council of Teachers of Mathematics (NCTM)—Principles and Standards for School Mathematics (http://standards.nctm.org)
- National Academies of Science (NAS)—National Science Education Standards (www.nap.edu/openbook.php?record_id=4962)
- National Center for History in the Schools and National Council for History Standards—National Standards for History (http://www.nchs.ucla.edu/Standards/)

Activity: Understanding Graphic Novels

To teach students and colleagues about graphic novels, this introductory activity uses two marvelous resources: *Maus: A Survivor's Tale* by Art Spiegelman and *Understanding Comics: The Invisible Art* by Scott McCloud. *Maus*, winner of a Pulitzer Prize in 1992, is a graphic novel about a serious topic—the Holocaust. McCloud's book is a fascinating, in-depth guide to all facets of cartoons and comics, and it is done completely in a comic format. Because of their legitimacy, these books are the gold standard to use when introducing graphic novels. Using *Maus*, participants learn about similarities between graphic novels and text-only novels; then, using *Understanding Comics*, they learn what makes graphic novels unique.

Books

An assortment of fiction and nonfiction graphic novels
Understanding Comics: The Invisible Art by Scott McCloud (HarperPerennial, 1994)
Maus: A Survivor's Tale by Art Spiegelman (Pantheon, 1986)

Materials

A document camera and data projector (or photocopied pages and an overhead projector)

Procedures/Activities

Have participants sit at tables with an assortment of graphic novels. Encourage participants to flip through the books while discussing these, or similar, questions:

- What do you know about comics and graphic novels?
- Why do comics appeal to people?
- What stereotypes are there about comics and the people who read them?

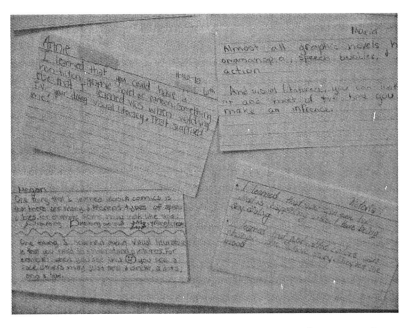

These cards provide a quick formative assessment of mastery after a unit on graphic novels.

Discuss a definition of graphic novels: "An original book-length story, either fiction or nonfiction, published in comic book style, or a collection of stories that have been published previously as individual comic books" (Gorman, 2003). "Graphic novel" refers to a format, not a genre!

Introduce participants to *Maus: A Survivor's Tale* by Art Spiegelman. Explain:

- Spiegelman studied and taught art and cartooning.
- His parents were survivors of the Auschwitz concentration camp and he wanted to tell their Holocaust story.
- He used the comic format because he felt comfortable with it.
- He interviewed his father and took 13 years to write the book.
- Maus was one of the first graphic novels.
- It tells two stories, one in the present and one in the past.

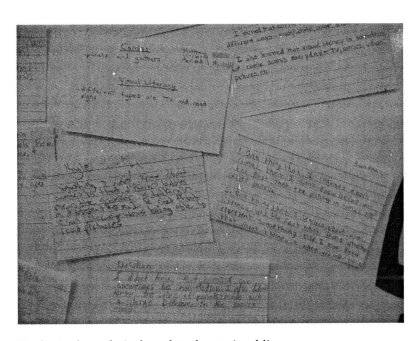

Students share their thoughts about visual literacy.

Teaching with Graphic Novels

There are a number of existing programs and websites developed to help educators who want to incorporate graphic novels into classroom instruction. These sites give tips on using graphic novels in an educational setting and offer sample lessons.

- *The Maryland Comic Book Initiative* http://www.marylandpublicschools.org/MSDE/programs/recognition-partnerships/md-comic-book
- *Reading With Pictures* http://www.readingwithpictures.org/Reading_With_Pictures/Home.html
- *Graphic Classroom* http://graphicclassroom.blogspot.com/
- *Comics in the Classroom* http://www.comicsintheclassroom.net/
- *Teachingcomics.org* http://www.teachingcomics.org/
- *Teaching Degree* http://www.teachingdegree.org/2009/07/05/comics-in-the-classroom-100-tips-tools-and-resources-for-teachers/
- *Lesson Planet* http://www.lessonplanet.com/search?keywords=graphic+novels&media=lesson

- Spiegelman portrayed Jews as mice and Nazis as cats.
- It won the Pulitzer Prize in 1992.

Discuss literary elements that are found in both print and graphic novels—characterization, setting, conflict, theme, style, tone, and mood.

Choose a page from *Maus* that illustrates characterization and display it using the document camera and projector or photocopies you have prepared. Ask participants:

- What can you tell about the characters?
- How does the author use speech, facial expression, point of view, action, and narration to help the reader learn about the characters?

Have participants use books on the tables to analyze characters in a similar way, comparing different types of graphic novels. Continue with other literary elements.

Use *Understanding Comics: The Invisible Art* by Scott McCloud to demonstrate and display comic elements and terms such as sequential art, panels, gutters, inference, transition, icons, and balloons.

Close with a discussion of these, or similar, questions:

- Do you have to read a graphic novel differently than a print novel?
- Which is more important in a graphic novel, text or illustrations?
- How does the artwork in the graphic novel reflect its topic?
- How does the artist's medium and style make it interdependent with the text?

Chapter 8

More Powerful Than a Locomotive: Teaching English Language Arts with Graphic Novels

Introduction

Fiction, nonfiction, classics, myths and legends, and genres. Rising action, symbolism, onomatopoeia, main idea. This is all typical content covered in English Language Arts classes, with many trusted resources on hand to teach these topics. Now you have a whole new arsenal available to you—graphic novels. Graphic novels lend themselves remarkably well to lessons in English Language Arts, not only for their powerful plots and masterful illustrations, but also for their literary devices, writing style, and vocabulary. Because graphic novels are—at heart—novels, they can be used interchangeably with text-only novels when planning a book study, a lesson on genre, or small group literature circle readings.

Graphic novels motivate readers who don't typically enjoy reading fiction. They deepen understanding by giving students context clues and visual representations of characters, settings, and unfamiliar vocabulary. When librarians and teachers use graphic novels with English language arts classes, students are actively involved and connected with books in a way they may not have been with traditional text-only novels.

The panels, gutters, narration, and voice bubbles in graphic novels can help students develop skills that are essential in reading comprehension. Determining main ideas and making inferences are important concepts taught in secondary English language arts. In fact, making inferences is like "reading" the gutters of a comic (McCloud, 2005). Students can perfect their reading strategies by using graphic novels to help them practice difficult skills like breaking passages into parts, asking themselves comprehension questions, and retelling what happened in the story. Graphic novels contain the same literary elements as text-only novels, making them valuable tools to use when teaching students to analyze characterization, setting, plot, theme, foreshadowing, and symbolism. Of course, before students can use the conventions of comic art as a framework to aid in reading comprehension, they will need that short lesson, on page 48, on Understanding Graphic Novels.

The ability to effectively read nonfiction is another important component of literacy and an essential skill that students must master for success in school. The illustrations in nonfiction graphic novels can help to facilitate students' comprehension of the information included, breaking the whole down into more manageable parts. Nonfiction books, however, are not only useful for gathering information. Many people, both adolescents and adults, prefer to read nonfiction for pleasure, too. The immense number of nonfiction graphic novels available today ensures that there are fascinating books for students that cover nearly all topics and interests.

Providing students with a wealth of reading materials for their reading pleasure is one of the best gifts librarians and teachers can give adolescents. To establish a culture of literacy within a school, students must have a considerable number of reading choices available. Providing students with time to read during the school day is another factor that helps students become better, more independent readers, and can help create life-long reading habits (Krashen, 1993). If you have incorporated a recreational reading program like Sustained Silent Reading (SSR) into your school day, you know that access to appealing reading material is crucial to a program's success (Pilgreen, 2000).

Graphic novels should be an integral part of the resources available for students' pleasure reading. Graphic novels can captivate readers of all abilities and developmental stages, and may include a "coolness" factor that appeals to many adolescents. The title and series lists in this chapter are longer than in other chapters because this list incorporates a large variety of fiction graphic novels that can be used for recreational reading. These books will captivate adolescents and help cultivate a love of reading. There are a large number of additional graphic novel titles that could have been included in this list. Due to space limitations, however, the lists have been limited to titles published since 2005.

References

Krashen, Stephen. *The Power of Reading*. Englewood, CO: Libraries Unlimited, 1993.
McCloud, Scott. *Understanding Comics*. New York: Harper Perennial, 1994.
Pilgreen, Janice L. *The SSR Handbook*. Portsmouth, NH: Heinemann, 2000.

Connecting to the Standards

AASL Standards for the 21st-Century Learner

4.1.2 Read widely and fluently to make connections with self, the world, and previous reading.

NCTE/IRA Standard for English Language Arts

Standard 3 Students apply a wide range of strategies to comprehend, interpret, evaluate, and appreciate texts. They draw on their prior experience, their interactions with other readers and writers, their knowledge of word meaning and of other texts, their word identification strategies, and their understanding of textual features (e.g., sound-letter correspondence, sentence structure, context, graphics).

The Bottom Line

Allowing students to read a variety of reading materials during free voluntary reading time—books, magazines, nonfiction, and graphic novels—makes reading a pleasure rather than a chore.

Comic Connections

- Allow students to create graphic novel panels as a book report option, using comic elements, such as panels, gutters, and voice balloons.
- Have students read a novel and then the graphic novel version, comparing and contrasting.
- Use graphic novels, especially manga, to illustrate onomatopoeia.
- Use Shaun Tan's *The Arrival* (Arthur A. Levine, 2007) to demonstrate symbolism.
- Have students read *Castle Waiting* by Linda Medley (Fantagraphic Books, 2006) or *Rapunzel's Revenge* by Shannon Hale and Dean Hale (Bloomsbury, 2008) to study common fairy tale elements.

Suggested Titles by Middle and High School (MS & HS)

Abadzis, Nick, and Hilary Sycamore. *Laika*. New York: First Second, 2007. (MS & HS)

Aristophane, and Matt Madden. *The Zabime Sisters*. New York: First Second, 2010. (HS)

Abel, Jessica, Gabriel Soria, and Warren Pleece. *Life Sucks*. New York: First Second, 2008. (HS)

Black, Holly, and Ted Naifeh. *The Good Neighbors*. New York: Graphix, 2008. (HS)

Brosgol, Vera. *Anya's Ghost*. New York: First Second, 2011. (MS & HS)

Busiek, Kurt, and David T. Wenzel. *The Wizard's Tale*. San Diego, CA: IDW Publishing, 2010. (MS)

Card, Orson S., Christopher Yost, Pasqual Ferry, Frank D'Armata, Cory Petit, and Jake Black. *Ender's Game: Battle School*. New York: Marvel Publishing Inc., 2009. (HS)

Carey, Mike, Sonny Liew, and Marc Hempel. *Re-gifters*. New York: DC Comics, 2007. (MS & HS)

Castellucci, Cecil, Jim Rugg, and Jared K. Fletcher. *The Plain Janes*. New York: Minx, 2007. (HS)

Chantler, Scott. *Tower of Treasure*. Toronto: Kids Can Press, 2010. (MS)

Clugston-Major, Chynna. *Queen Bee*. New York: Graphix, 2005. (MS)

Davis, Eleanor. *The Secret Science Alliance and the Copycat Crook*. New York: Bloomsbury, 2009. (MS)

Deutsch, Barry. *Hereville: How Mirka Got Her Sword*. New York: Amulet, 2010. (MS)

Fies, Brian. *Mom's Cancer*. New York: Abrams Image, 2006. (MS & HS)

Gipi. *Garage Band*. New York: First Second, 2007. (HS)

Gillis, Peter B. *The Last Unicorn*. San Diego, CA: IDW, 2011. (MS & HS)

Gulledge, Laura Lee. *Page by Paige*. New York: Amulet Books, 2011. (MS & HS)

Hale, Shannon, Dean Hale, and Nathan Hale. *Calamity Jack*. New York: Bloomsbury, 2010. (MS)

Hale, Shannon, Dean Hale, and Nathan Hale. *Rapunzel's Revenge*. New York: Bloomsbury, 2008. (MS)

Hamilton, Tim, and Ray Bradbury. *Ray Bradbury's Fahrenheit 451: The Authorized Adaptation*. New York: Hill and Wang, 2009. (MS & HS)

Harrison, Lisi, and Yishan Li. *The Clique: a Graphic Novel*. New York: Yen Press, 2010. (MS)

Hicks, Faith E. *The War at Ellsmere*. San Jose, CA: SLG Pub, 2008. (MS)

Higson, Charles, Kev Walker, and Ian Fleming. *Silverfin: The Graphic Novel*. New York: Disney-Hyperion Books, 2010. (MS & HS)

Jablonski, Carla, Leland Purvis, and Hilary Sycamore. *Resistance: Book 1*. New York: First Second, 2010. (MS)

Jacobson, Sidney, and Ernie Colón. *Anne Frank: The Anne Frank House Authorized Graphic Biography*. New York: Hill and Wang, 2010. (MS & HS)

Jacques, Brian, Bret Blevins, Stuart Moore, and Richard Starkings. *Redwall: The Graphic Novel*. New York: Philomel Books, 2007. (MS)

Jones, Gerard, and Mark Badger. *Networked: Carabella on the Run*. New York: Privacy Activism/NBM Publishing, 2010. (HS)

Kelly, Joe, and Max Fiumara. *Four Eyes*. Berkeley, CA: Image Comics, 2010. (HS)

Kibuishi, Kazu. *Copper*. New York: Graphix/Scholastic, 2010. (MS)

Kim, Susan, Laurence Klavan, and Faith E. Hicks. *Brain Camp*. New York: First Second, 2010. (MS)

Kovac, Tommy, Lewis Carroll, and Sonny Liew. *Wonderland*. New York: Disney Press, 2008. (MS)

Larson, Hope. *Mercury*. New York: Atheneum Books for Young Readers, 2010. (HS)

Lat. *Kampung Boy*. New York: First Second, 2006. (MS)

Lat. *Town Boy*. New York: First Second, 2007. (MS)

Lemire, Jeff, and H. G. Wells. *The Nobody*. New York: Vertigo, 2009. (HS)

Love, Jeremy, and Patrick Morgan. *Bayou: Volume One*. New York: DC Comics, 2009. (HS)

McCann, Jim, and Janet Lee. *The Return of the Dapper Men*. Los Angeles: Archaia Comics, 2010. (MS)

Mechner, Jordan, LeUyen Pham, and Alex Puvilland. *Solomon's Thieves: Book One*. New York: First Second, 2010. (HS)

Neri, G. *Yummy: The Last Days of a Southside Shorty*. New York: Lee & Low Books, 2010. (MS & HS)

Novgorodoff, Danica, James Ponsoldt, Benjamin Percy, and Hilary Sycamore. *Refresh, Refresh: A Graphic Novel*. New York: First Second, 2009. (HS)

Novgorodoff, Danica. *Slow Storm*. New York: First Second, 2008. (HS)

O'Donnell, Liam, and Mike Deas. *Ramp Rats: A Graphic Guide Adventure*. Victoria, BC: Orca Book Publishers, 2008. (MS)

Phelan, Matt. *The Storm in the Barn*. Somerville, MA: Candlewick Press, 2009. (MS)

Pink, Daniel H., and Pas R. Ten. *The Adventures of Johnny Bunko: The Last Career Guide You'll Ever Need*. New York: Riverhead Books, 2008. (HS)

Powell, Nate. *Swallow Me Whole*. Marietta, GA: Top Shelf, 2008. (HS)

Pyle, Kevin C. *Blindspot*. New York: H. Holt, 2007. (MS)

Renier, Aaron, and Alec Longstreth. *The Unsinkable Walker Bean*. New York: First Second, 2010. (MS & HS)

Riordan, Rick, Robert Venditti, Attila Futaki, and Josè Villarrubia. *The Lightning Thief: The Graphic Novel*. New York: Disney/Hyperion Books, 2010. (MS)

Russell, P. Craig. *Coraline*. New York: HarperCollins, 2008. (MS)

Sala, Richard. *Cat Burglar Black*. New York: First Second, 2009. (MS)

Sfar, Joann, Antoine de Saint-Exupéry, and Brigitte Findakly. *The Little Prince*. Boston: Houghton Mifflin Harcourt, 2010. (HS)

Shanower, Eric, L. F. Baum, and Skottie Young. *The Wonderful Wizard of Oz*. New York: Marvel Publishing Inc., 2009. (MS)

Shiga, Jason. *Meanwhile*. New York: Amulet Books, 2010. (MS)

Siegel, Siena C., and Mark Siegel. *To Dance: A Memoir*. New York: Atheneum Books for Young Readers, 2006. (MS)

Sina, A. B., LeUyen Pham, Alex Puvilland, and Jordan Mechner. *Prince of Persia, the Graphic Novel*. New York: First Second, 2008. (HS)

Small, David. *Stitches: A Memoir*. New York: W.W. Norton & Co, 2009. (HS)

Smith, Jeff, and Charles Vess. *Rose*. New York: Graphix, 2009. (MS & HS)

Spiegelman, Art, and Françoise Mouly. *Big Fat Little Lit*. New York: Puffin, 2006. (MS)

Steinberger, Aimee M. *Japan Ai: A Tall Girl's Adventures in Japan*. Agoura Hills, CA: Go! Comi, 2007. (HS)

Sturm, James, Andrew Arnold, and Alexis Frederick-Frost. *Adventures in Cartooning*. New York: First Second, 2009. (MS)

Tamaki, Mariko, and Jillian Tamaki. *Skim*. Toronto: Groundwood Books, 2008. (HS)

Tan, Shaun. *The Arrival*. New York: Arthur A. Levine Books, 2007. (MS & HS)

Tan, Shaun. *Tales from Outer Suburbia*. New York: Arthur A. Levine Books, 2009. (MS & HS)

Telgemeier, Raina. *Smile*. New York: Graphix, 2010. (MS)

TenNapel, Doug, and Chris Staros. *Creature Tech*. Marietta, GA: Top Shelf Productions, 2010. (HS)

TenNapel, Doug. *Ghostopolis*. New York: Graphix/Scholastic, 2010. (MS)

Vachss, Andrew H., Frank T. Caruso, and Zak Mucha. *Heart Transplant*. Milwaukie, OR: Dark Horse, 2010. (HS)

Varon, Sara. *Robot Dreams*. New York: First Second, 2007. (MS)

Vaughan, Brian K., Niko Henrichon, and Todd Klein. *Pride of Baghdad*. New York: DC Comics, 2006. (HS)

Weing, Drew. *Set to Sea*. Seattle, WA: Fantagraphics, 2010. (MS & HS)

Weinstein, Lauren R. *Girl Stories*. New York: Henry Holt, 2006. (MS)

White, Tracy. *How I Made It to Eighteen: A Mostly True Story*. New York: Roaring Brook Press, 2010. (HS)

Wilson, G. W., and M. K. Perker. *Cairo: A Graphic Novel*. New York: DC Comics, 2007. (HS)

Wood, Don. *Into the Volcano: A Graphic Novel*. New York: The Blue Sky Press, 2008. (MS)

Yang, Gene L., and Lark Pien. *American Born Chinese*. New York: First Second, 2006. (MS & HS)

Yang, Gene L., and Derek K. Kim. *The Eternal Smile: Three Stories*. New York: First Second, 2009. (HS)

Yang, Gene L., and Thien Pham. *Level Up*. New York: First Second, 2011. (HS)

Yang, Gene L. *Prime Baby*. New York: First Second, 2010. (MS)

Yolen, Jane, and Michael Cavallaro. *Foiled*. New York: First Second, 2010. (MS & HS)

Suggested Titles in a Series

Bannister, Art, and Nykko. *The Elsewhere Chronicles* Series. Minneapolis, MN: Graphic Universe. (MS)

Colfer, Eoin. *Artemis Fowl* Series. New York: Miramax Books/Hyperion Books for Children. (MS)

Crilley, Mark. *Brody's Ghost* Series. Milwaukie, OR: Dark Horse Books. (MS & HS)

Gaiman, Neil. *The Sandman* Series. New York: Vertigo. (HS)

Geary, Rick. *Treasury of Victorian Murder* Series. New York: NBM ComicsLit. (HS)

Halo Series. New York: Marvel Pub. (HS)

Higgins, Dusty, and Van Jensen. *Pinocchio Vampire Slayer* Series. San Jose, CA: SLG. (HS)

Horowitz, Anthony. *The Alex Rider Graphic* Series. New York: Philomel. (MS)

Igarashi, Daisuke. *Children of the Sea* Series. San Francisco, CA: Viz Media. (MS & HS)

Jolley, Dan, and Erin Hunter. *Warriors* Series. Hamburg: Tokyopop. (MS)

Kibuishi, Kazu. *Flight* Series. New York: Villard Books. (MS & HS)

Kim, Young, and Stephenie Meyer. *Twilight: The Graphic Novel*. New York: Yen Press, 2010. (MS & HS)

Kneece, Mark, and Rod Serling. *The Twilight Zone* Series. New York: Walker & Co. (MS)

Knaak, Richard A., and Chae-hwan Kim. *Warcraft the Sunwell Trilogy* Series. Hamburg: Tokyopop. (HS)

Lagos, Alexander, Joseph Lagos, and Steve J. Walker. *The Sons of Liberty* Series. New York: Random House Children's Books. (MS & HS)

Lewis, J. S., Jon Buran, Oliver Nome, and Allen Martinez. *Free Realms* Series. La Jolla, CA: WildStorm Productions. (MS & HS)

Lobdell, Scott. *The Hardy Boys* Series. New York: Papercutz. (MS)

Mariolle, Mathieu, MiniKim, and Pop. *Nola's Worlds* Series. Minneapolis, MN: Graphic Universe, 2010. (MS)

Medley, Linda. *Castle Waiting* Series. Seattle, WA: Fantagraphics. (MS & HS)

Nicolle, Malachai, and Ethan Nicolle. *Axe Cop* Series. Milwaukie, OR: Dark Horse, 2011. (HS)

Naifeh, Ted. *Courtney Crumrin* Series. Portland, OR: ONI Press. (MS)

O'Connor, George. *Olympians (Athena, Zeus)* Series. New York: First Second. (MS)

O'Malley, Bryan L. *Scott Pilgrim* Series. Portland, OR: Oni Press. (HS)

Petersen, David. *Mouse Guard* Series. Los Angeles, CA: Archaia Entertainment. (MS)

Petrucha, Stefan. *Nancy Drew* Series. New York: Papercutz. (MS)

Robbins, Trina, and Tyler Page. *Chicagoland Detective Agency* Series. Minneapolis, MN: Graphic Universe. (MS)

Schweizer, Chris. *Crogan's* Series. Portland, OR: Oni Press. (MS & HS)

Siddell, Tom. *Gunnerkrigg Court* Series. Fort Lee, NJ: Archaia Studios Press. (MS)

Smith, Jeff. *Bone* Series. New York, NY: Graphix/Scholastic. (MS & HS)

Stine, R. L. *Goosebumps* Graphic Series. New York: Scholastic. (MS)

Stroud, Jonathan. *The Bartimaeus* Series. New York: Miramax Books/Hyperion. (MS)

Telgemeier, Raina, and Ann M. Martin. *Baby-sitter's Club* Graphic Series. New York: Graphix. (MS)

Tsang, Evonne, and Janina Görrissen. *My Boyfriend is a Monster* Series. Minneapolis, MN: Graphic Universe. (MS & HS)

Venditti, Robert. *Percy Jackson and the Olympians* Series. New York: Hyperion. (MS)

Wilson, Seán Michael, and Chie Kutsuwada. *The Story of Lee* Series. New York: NBM Comics Lit., 2010. (HS)

Lesson Plans

Lesson Plan Title: Evaluating Graphic Novels

Grade Level: MS, HS

Subject Area: English Language Arts

Curriculum Focus/Concepts: Developing reading strategies, literary elements, evaluating literature.

Graphic Novel Tie-In:

Fiction graphic novels include the same literary devices that text-only novels contain. Graphic novels, with their panels and the context clues in the illustrations, can make these literary elements simpler to find. After receiving instruction on the literary elements of fiction, each student will read a fiction graphic novel of their choice. Using the Graphic Novel Evaluation Form for guidelines on identifying literary elements like characterization, setting, plot, style, mood, and tone, they will identify and analyze these story elements. You can adjust these topics depending on your instruction and what you want students to know. Be sure to include prior instruction on how to read graphic novels, using the Understanding Graphic Novel lesson on page 48 of this book.

Objectives:
Students will utilize reading strategies for understanding.
Students will identify and explain story elements.
Students will critically analyze literature.
Students will give reasons and cite examples from text to support opinions.

Materials/Resources:
Books
One fiction graphic novel for each student

Materials
Graphic Novel Evaluation Form

Procedures/Activities:
Have students read a fiction graphic novel of their choice, and then complete the Graphic Novel Evaluation Form.

Discussion Questions:
How is reading a graphic novel different from reading a text-only novel?
How does the artwork in the graphic novel reflect its topic?
How does the artist's medium and style make the art interdependent with the text?

Closure:
Have students create booktalks or book trailers for their graphic novels, describing some of the literary elements while generating interest in the various titles.

Extension Activities:
Have students read about the authors of their graphic novels, using resources such as:

- *Graphic Novelists: Profiles of Cutting Edge Authors and Illustrators* by Tom and Sara Pendergast (UXL, 2007)
- The *Library of Graphic Novelists* series (Rosen, 2005)
- :01 First Second Creators (http://us.macmillan.com/Content.aspx?publisher=firstsecond&id=5695)

- Authors at HarperCollins Publishers (http://www.harpercollins.com/Author/Browse.aspx)
- Individual graphic novelists' websites

Assessment:
Grade the Graphic Novel Evaluation Form, the booktalks, and any products students created about their authors.

Graphic Novel Evaluation Form

Characterization

- List at least 3 characters' names.
- How does the author use speech, facial expression, action and narration to explain each character?

1.
2.
3.

Setting

- Where does the story take place?
- What time period is involved?
- What is the environment like?
- What clues do the art give you about the setting?

Plot Development

- Summarize what happens in the beginning, the middle and the end of the story.
- Is it easy to follow and does it make sense? Explain your answer.
- Discuss the conflict in the story. How is it resolved?

Graphic Style

- How does color (or lack of it) in the illustrations add to the story?
- Why do you think the author drew the illustrations the way he or she did?
- How did the author use panels, gutters, and voice balloons to add interest or advance the story?

Mood and Tone

- What is the overall mood and tone of the book (humorous, dark, romantic, angry, etc.)?
- How does the author use the text and art to achieve this tone?
- What makes this book unique?

What did you like best about the book? What did you like least?

Lesson Plan Title: Literature Circles Go Graphic

Grade Level: MS and HS

Subject Area: English Language Arts

Curriculum Focus/Concepts: Develop reading strategies, analyze story elements, critically evaluate literature

Graphic Novel Tie-In:

In literature circle reading groups, students read the same book as a small group and then collaborate while discussing the book and their reactions to it. Groups are student-led and all participants play a vital role. Through literature circles, students develop critical thinking skills, work together to derive deeper understanding of what they read, and are responsible for their own learning. Students tend to enjoy literature circles and are motivated to make them successful.

By introducing graphic novels into a program of literature circles, students can evaluate a novel's merits in new ways—considering the art as well as the text—while analyzing such elements as plot, characterization, and setting.

Because book choice is a crucial part of literature circle reading, four or five copies of each graphic title must be available. Any graphic novel titles will work, as long as a selection of genres, reading levels, and subjects is given to provide for differentiated instruction. Because graphic novels generally include less text than other novels, this project may not take as long as traditional literature circle readings. Students can probably finish their books in a week or so.

Objectives:
Students will use criteria to choose a graphic novel to read.
Students will analyze elements such as plot, theme, characterization, and setting.
Students will express their opinions about the format and content of graphic novels.
Students will collaborate in literature circle groups.

Materials/Resources:
Books
Sets of graphic novels copies, offering a selection of genres, reading levels, and subjects

Materials
Literature circle lesson plan and rubric, either your own or one from these sites:
ReadWriteThink (http://www.readwritethink.org/)
Education World (http://www.educationworld.com/)

Procedures/Activities
Teach students the basics of graphic novels and comic art with the Understanding Graphic Novels lesson on page 48.
Allow students to choose a book that interests them and form their literature circles.
Explain literature circle reading groups, the participants' roles, and the expectations.

Have students sit with their groups, divide the chapters or pages to be read over a specific period of time, discuss roles, and begin reading.

Stress to students that they need to read their graphic novels in a slow, deliberate way, enriching understanding by "reading" the art as well as the text.

Discussion Questions:

Did you have to read this book in a different way than you are used to? What did you have to do differently?

Compared to other books you've read, was the graphic novel easier to understand, or harder? Why?

What did you like about reading a graphic novel? What did you dislike?

How does the artwork in the graphic novel reflect its topic?

How does the artist's medium and style make the art interdependent with the text?

Closure:

Have students discuss their feelings about reading graphic novels; what they liked and didn't like, their favorite and least favorite parts about their graphic novels, and whether or not they think they will read other graphic novels.

Extension Activities:

Have students give group presentations about their books.

Assessment:

Assess any worksheets your students completed as they read, and the group presentations.

Lesson Plan Title: Main Ideas and Making Inferences

Grade Level: MS, HS

Subject Area: English Language Arts

Curriculum Focus/Concepts: Reading strategies, comprehension, thinking skills

Graphic Novel Tie-In:

From the time they are beginning readers, students are taught to find the main ideas in what they read, as a way of understanding an overlying theme, and as an important comprehension skill. Making inferences and drawing conclusions are other essential reading comprehension skills. Sequential art helps students identify main ideas. The discrete panels in graphic novels break stories down into parts, making it easier to determine what is important. And, since the amount of text in a graphic novel is usually limited, every word is important. For example, an author may need a paragraph to describe a scene, where a graphic novelist can depict the same scene in one panel.

Correspondingly, the gutters in sequential art force a reader to make inferences. In a similar way that students "read between the lines" of text, readers of comics use clues in the panels to imagine what is happening between the panels, or in the gutters. By understanding what strategies they are using when reading comics, students can become better adept at using these same skills of inference and deduction in all their reading.

This group of students is making inferences, using the text and sequential art in graphic novels.

Objectives:
Students will develop strategies for improved reading comprehension.
Students will determine the main ideas of what they read.
Students will draw conclusions and inferences for deeper understanding.

Materials/Resources:
Books
A graphic novel for each student or group of students.

Procedures/Activities:
Teach students the basics of graphic novels and comic art with the Understanding Graphic Novels lesson on page 48.
Have students read and analyze, individually or in groups, a page or chapter from a graphic novel.
Instruct students to make a list of the main idea(s) of their page or chapter, citing evidence from the text.
Students should then list inferences they made during their reading, making certain these inferences are not stated in the graphic novel, but are feelings they get or deductions they make from the illustrations.

Discussion Questions:
How did you determine the main ideas in your graphic novel?
What clues did you find to support your decision?
What inferences did you make?
What clues did you find in the graphic novel to help you make inferences?
How did the author/artist use both text and art to convey main idea?
How did the author/artist use panels and gutters to help make inferences?

Closure: Discuss as a class how students can use these same skills in their future readings.

Extension Activities:
After the activity, give students short text-only passages to practice the same skills.

Assessment:
Assess the students on their participation in the group work, and their understanding of these literary skills.

Lesson Plan Title: From Nonfiction to Art

Grade Level: MS, HS

Subject Areas: English Language Arts, Writing, Art

Curriculum Focus/Concepts: Reading informational materials, critical thinking, drawing.

Graphic Novel Tie-In:
Reading and understanding nonfiction writing is one of the most important skills students can master. It is a crucial part of conducting research, comprehending textbooks, and seeking information on topics of personal interest. As they prepare to write reports, students must determine what to include, structure information into logical parts, and put them into an appropriate sequence of events.

Creating graphic panels from nonfiction text supports comprehension. Drawing helps students visualize and grasp main ideas. It serves much the same purpose as an outline, while offering a creative component that's appealing. Writing text, in the form of dialogue and narration, forces students to write concisely, making every word count.

Even students who have little artistic talent can draw comic panels. Stick figures are acceptable—the content is what is important. Make sure students have had an introductory lesson on comic art, with an understanding of panels, gutters, and other comic elements.

Objectives:
Students will analyze factual information.
Students will identify key points and important details.
Students will organize information, creating an outline and report on a topic.
Students will create a graphic product.

Materials/Resources:
Materials
A variety of nonfiction articles/books written at varying levels appropriate for students. Topics can be related to subjects currently studied, or high-interest topics suitable for personal information-gathering.
Sundays comics sections, cut into separate strips. Cut each strip into individual panels, with each strip stored in an envelope or zipper bag.
Paper, pencils, markers, colored pencils, and so on for creating comic panels.

Procedures/Activities

Students choose and read a nonfiction book, after jotting down notes about prior knowledge of their topics and what they want to learn.

While reading, students should take notes on what they find important, write down key vocabulary words, and pull out main ideas and supporting details. They then should organize those notes into a logical sequence, using note cards. These note cards will later become their "storyboards."

After nonfiction reading is finished, give each student one of the cut-up comics. Have them put the strips together in the correct order, to practice sequencing.

Have students create their own graphic panels to depict the content of their articles/ books.

Have students write a reflection of the activity in 2–3 paragraphs.

Discussion Questions:

How did you decide what order your panels should be placed in?

Was drawing your own graphic novel easier or harder than you expected? What was easiest? What was most difficult?

What are some advantages of reading graphic nonfiction? What are some disadvantages?

Closure:

Lead the class in a discussion of visual literacy: what it is, why it's important, how it can help in writing, how it can add interest and deepen understanding of what we read and view.

Extension Activities:

Have students share their projects with one another.

Assessment:

Assess the students' work through the use of a rubric.

Chapter 9

The Write Stuff: Teaching Writing with Graphic Novels

Introduction

Graphic novels serve as excellent writing prompts for students. There is a world of writing potential in sequential art, where each panel is packed with rich visual details and crisp text. Graphic panels are waiting for readers to bring their imaginations into the story as they interpret the plot, fill in missing pieces, and predict what will come next.

Good stories require much of a reader. Readers bring their prior knowledge and interpretive skills into a story. Often, that is what makes a story especially compelling to a reader and is why two people can read the same narrative and come away with drastically different impressions. Wordless graphic novels such as Shaun Tan's *The Arrival* (2006) or *Robot Dreams* by Sara Varon (2007) illustrate this concept perfectly. These books offer exceptional imaginative and interpretive experiences for readers.

Reading graphic novels can help students break their own writing down into parts. In a graphic novel, each panel, each voice bubble, and every detail of the art is a separate component of the writing. Sequential art, in its basic form, is organized and linear. One panel clearly leads to the next and builds upon preceding panels. For some students, graphic novels may help them learn to identify main ideas, supporting details, and important changes in the plot line.

All authors strive for strong, polished writing. Writing text for comics forces a writer to be concise and edit wordy writing, making it more precise and powerful. As students' writing becomes longer and more sophisticated, an understanding of sequential art can help them create their own methods of organizing and editing their writing, whether it is through graphic organizers, outlines, or a type of writing storyboard. Using the same tools creators of graphic novels use can help students become better writers.

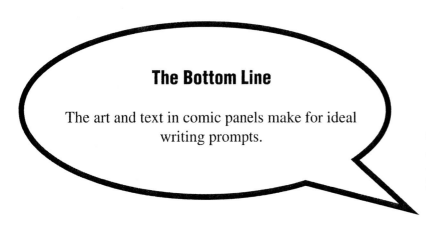

The Bottom Line

The art and text in comic panels make for ideal writing prompts.

Connecting to the Standards

AASL Standards for the 21st-Century Learner

2.1.6 Use the writing process, media and visual literacy, and technology skills to create products that express new understandings.

NCTE/IRA Standard for English Language Arts

Standard 5. Students employ a wide range of strategies as they write and use different writing process elements appropriately to communicate with different audiences for a variety of purposes.

Comic Connections

- Provide students with several panels from a comic with the voice bubbles empty. Have students write their own dialogue, then compare with what others wrote, discussing how each reader interpreted the panels differently.
- After reading graphic novels, have students write diary entries from the main character's point of view.
- Use Richard A. Knaak's *WarCraft* series graphic novels to help teach SAT vocabulary words.
- Give students one panel from a graphic novel, featuring at least one character. Have students write a paragraph, describing the character's physical appearance, using descriptive language.
- After reading a page from a graphic novel, instruct students to write down what they learned about the story from only the art, and what they learned from just the text. Have them explain how the art and text worked interdependently to tell the story.
- When teaching a unit on argumentative or persuasive writing, use Neri's *Yummy: The Last Days of a Southside Shorty*, a powerful story of a gang shooting, to demonstrate to students how to focus on an important issue, learn about both sides of the issue, and come up with possible solutions.

Suggested Titles by Middle and High School (MS & HS)

Neri, G. *Yummy: The Last Days of a Southside Shorty*. New York: Lee & Low Books, 2010. (MS & HS)

Tan, Shaun. *The Arrival*. New York: Arthur A. Levine, 2006. (MS & HS)

Varon, Sara. *Robot Dreams*. New York: First Second, 2007. (MS)

Suggested Titles in a Series

Knaak, Richard A. *Warcraft: the Sunwell Triology. Volume 1, Dragon Hunt.* Los Angeles: Tokyopop, 2007. (HS)

Knaak, Richard A. *Warcraft: the Sunwell Triology. Volume 2, Shadows of Ice.* Los Angeles: Tokyopop, 2007. (HS)

Slade, Christian. *Korgi: Book 1, Sprouting Wings.* Portland, OR: Top Shelf Productions, 2007. (MS)

Slade, Christian. *Korgi: Book 2, The Cosmic Collector.* Portland, OR: Top Shelf Productions, 2008. (MS)

Lesson Plans

Lesson Plan Title: Interpreting Wordless Graphic Novels

Grade Level: MS, HS

Subject Areas: English Language Arts, Writing

Curriculum Focus/Concepts: Literary elements, narrative writing, inference and interpretation

Graphic Novel Tie-In:

Wordless graphic novels such as *The Arrival* by Shaun Tan, *Korgi* by Christian Slade, and *Robot Dreams* by Sara Varon allow students' imaginations free reign when they interpret the story through art alone. They must supply their own interpretation of the characters' motivations and thoughts, dialogue, and plot.

Each reader sees a book through the filter of his own previous experiences, so no two readers will interpret a wordless graphic novel in quite the same way. This makes these books excellent writing prompts for narrative writing. The goal of the assignment is a piece of polished, sophisticated narration, unique to each writer.

Objectives:

Students will develop reading strategies.

Students will interpret and analyze literary elements such as setting, character, plot, and symbolism.

Students will make inferences and draw conclusions.

Students will evaluate author's voice, and its effects on the reader.

Students will effectively use language, grammar, punctuation, and vocabulary to create author's voice in a narrative.

Materials/Resources:

Books

Slade, Christian. *Korgi: Book 1, Sprouting Wings.* Portland, OR: Top Shelf Productions, 2007.

Tan, Shaun. *The Arrival.* New York: Arthur A. Levine, 2006.

Varon, Sara. *Robot Dreams.* New York: First Second, 2007.

Procedures/Activities:
Have students read all, or portions of, the graphic novels listed above.
Have students write a piece of narrative writing, based on the stories in the books, including descriptions of the setting, and the characters' traits and thoughts. Students should create dialogue, interpret and explain subjective parts of the stories, and describe the meaning of any symbolism involved.

Discussion Questions:
What reasons would an author have for creating a book for older readers that has no text?
How do these graphic novels manage to include dialogue without any words?
How does the author convey the characters' traits through only art?
Was it easy or hard to interpret this wordless story? Why?
How does the artwork in the graphic novel reflect its topic?
How does the artist's medium and style convey voice and mood?

Closure: Have the students read their stories, discussing their differences and why readers interpret stories in various ways.

Extension Activities: Have students create their own wordless stories in comic panels.

Assessment: Assess the students' narrative writing.

Lesson Plan Title: From Art to Description

Grade Level: MS, HS

Subject Areas: English Language Arts, Writing

Curriculum Focus/Concepts: Descriptive writing, inference and interpretation

Graphic Novel Tie-In:
Creativity and detail add richness to the artwork within graphic novels. Color, shading, style, and technique give the art a unique "feel" that is specific to an artist. Vivid writing full of sensory detail gives a similar "feel" to descriptive writing. By writing a description of the panels in a graphic novel, students can use the art and text to put the story into narrative form, adding their own details.
Panels from any graphic novel can be used for this lesson. An assortment of books with artwork in different styles will allow students to choose a book they will enjoy and appreciate. Rich description using the five senses should be included in students' writing, with a short, polished piece of creative writing as the final product.

Objectives:
Students will respond creatively to written and visual stories.
Students will critically interpret literature.
Students will analyze literary elements.

Students will effectively use language, grammar, punctuation, and vocabulary to create author's voice in a narrative.

Materials/Resources:
Books
An assortment of graphic novels, allowing one per student.

Procedure/Activities:
Have students browse through a graphic novel and choose a portion of it to write about, with the size of the portion and the length of the writing determined by the teacher.
Students then write about the panels, describing the characters and their feelings, as well as the setting, plot, and action.
Students should use descriptive language, including the five senses.
Students should use the narration in the graphic panels as main ideas, and create dialogue for the characters from the voice bubbles.
Panels should be represented as paragraphs.

Discussion Questions:
What part of the comic conveys the sounds, sights, smells, and feelings you included in your writing?
How does the author/artist depict mood, tone and style through the images? How did you convert this into text?
Did you include parts in your writing that took place "in the gutter" of the graphic novel? Why?
How does the artwork in the graphic novel reflect its topic?
How does the artist's medium and style make it interdependent with the text?

Closure: Have students pair up and read one another's work.

Extension Activities:
Have students write a narrative of the same graphic novel story from the perspective of the main character and told in first person.

Assessment:
Assess the students' writing for structure, content, and adherence to conventions.

Chapter 10

Connecting with the Classics: Graphic Novel Adaptations

Introduction

A classic is something that everybody wants to have read and nobody wants to read.

—Twain, 1900

Mark Twain's quote may have been true for his time; however, the literary world has changed dramatically over the past 100 years. It is far less intimidating to read the classics these days, thanks to the combination of art and text found in graphic novel adaptations. There has been exponential growth in the number of classic adaptations offered in the graphic novel format, over the past five to ten years alone. In addition, librarians and teachers are quickly realizing that graphic novel adaptations can serve a variety of functions for a variety of readers. The sequential art in graphic novels can help a wide range of readers develop an appreciation for classic literature that they might not experience otherwise. For reluctant readers and second language learners, reading the graphic novel versions of classics may be the first time they have been exposed to a particular title or author. The engaging illustrations are a means of exposing them to visual adaptations of the literary canon. The graphic novel adaptation of a classic can also help second language learners and struggling readers grasp the story line.

Reading the graphic novel counterpart of a classic title may inspire a reader to move on to the original version. One reason many teachers use graphic novels in the classroom is to steer students toward more prose-oriented texts such as the classics (Frey & Fisher, 2008). For students reading on grade level and more advanced readers, graphic adaptations can provide them with some background before they read the original version of a classic. For example, Advanced Placement (AP) and other English Language Arts (ELA) teachers can use the graphic novel versions of *Beowulf* (Hinds, 2007; Storrie & Randall, (2008) to help students comprehend the alliterative verse, and view the epic poem in new and different ways.

References

Frey, Nancy and Fisher, Doug. *Teaching Visual Literacy: Using Comic Books, Graphic Novels, Anime, Cartoons, and More to Develop Comprehension and Thinking Skills.* Thousand Oaks, CA: Corwin Press, 2008.

Hinds, Gareth. *Beowulf.* Cambridge, MA: Candlewick Press, 2007.

Storrie, Paul D., and Ron Randall. 2009. *Beowulf: monster slayer. Graphic universe.* London: Lerner.

Twain, Mark. *Quotations Page.* http://www.quotationspage.com/quote/172.html (cited January 26, 2010).

Connecting to the Standards

AASL Standards for the 21st-Century Learner

4.1.2 Read widely and fluently to make connections with self, the world, and previous reading.

4.1.3 Respond to literature and creative expressions of ideas in various formats and genres.

NCTE/IRA Standard for English Language Arts

Standard 3 Students apply a wide range of strategies to comprehend, interpret, evaluate, and appreciate texts. They draw on their prior experience, their interactions with other readers and writers, their knowledge of word meaning and of other texts, their word identification strategies, and their understanding of textual features (e.g., sound-letter correspondence, sentence structure, context, graphics).

Comic Connections

- There are a variety of graphic novel adaptations of the Sherlock Holmes mysteries. Use some of the following adaptations as part of a unit on Sir Arthur Conan Doyle and his famous detective:

  Doyle, Sir Arthur. *A Study in Scarlet: A Sherlock Holmes Graphic Novel.* Adapted by Ian Edginton and illustrated by I. N. J. Culbard. Illustrated Classics Ser. New York: Sterling Publishing, 2010.

  Doyle, Arthur. *Sherlock Holmes, Volume 1.* Adapted and illustrated by Kelly Jones. San Diego, CA: IDW Publishing, 2009. (MS & HS) * There are two other volumes in this series.

  Doyle, Sir Arthur. *The Adventure of the Dancing Men.* Adapted by Vincent Goodwin and illustrated by Ben Dunn. Graphic Novel Adventures of Sherlock Holmes Ser. Minneapolis, MN: ABDO Publishing, 2010. *Other titles in the series include, *The Adventure of the Empty House, The Adventure of the Norwood Builder, The Adventure of the Red-Headed League, and The Adventure of Abby Grange.*

  Middle school students will enjoy the Sherlock Holmes web quest located at http://www.interacting.info/old/Level%202/2-3.shows_young_sec/sherlock/SherlockWQ.pdf.

- Marvel Illustrated Classics provides teacher's guides for their classics, *Man in the Iron Mask, Last of the Mohicans*, and *Treasure Island*. You can download these PDF files at: http://marvel.com/comics/Marvel_Illustrated

The Bottom Line

Graphic novel adaptations of the classics allow for differentiated instruction by meeting the needs of a wide variety of learners, from struggling readers to those who are college bound.

Suggested Titles by Middle and High School (MS & HS)

The following is a list of graphic novel renditions of classics that can introduce students to the classics and/or enhance their understanding of them. Titles in a series will be listed by publisher below individually listed titles.

Beowulf. Adapted and illustrated by Gareth Hinds. Cambridge, MA: Candlewick Press, 2007. (HS)

Cervantes, Miguel De. *The Last Knight.* Adapted and illustrated by Will Eisner. New York: NBM Publishing, 2000. (MS)

Dante's Devine Comedy: A Graphic Adaptation. Adapted and illustrated by Seymour Chwast. New York: Bloomsbury USA, 2010. (HS)

Defoe, Daniel. *Robinson Crusoe.* Adapted and illustrated by Jean-Christophe Vergne. San Diego, CA: IDW Publishing, 2009. (HS)

Dickens, Charles. *A Christmas Carol.* Adapted by Patrice Buendia and illustrated by Jean-Marc Stalner. San Diego, CA: IDW Publishing, 2009. (HS)

Dickens, Charles. *Oliver Twist.* Adapted by David Cerquiera and illustrated by Philippe Chanoinat. San Diego, CA: IDW Publishing, 2009. (HS)

Doyle, Arthur. *Sherlock Holmes, Vol 1.* Adapted and illustrated by Kelly Jones. San Diego, CA: IDW Publishing, 2009. (MS & HS)

Doyle, Arthur. *Sherlock Holmes, Vol 2.* Adapted and illustrated by Kelly Jones. San Diego, CA: IDW Publishing, 2010. (MS & HS)

Doyle, Arthur. *Sherlock Holmes, Vol 3.* Adapted and illustrated by Kelly Jones. San Diego, CA: IDW Publishing, 2010. (MS & HS)

Excalibur: The Legend of King Arthur. Adapted by Tony Lee & illustrated by Sam Hart. Cambridge, MA: Candlewick Press, 2011. (MS & HS)

Homer. *The Odyssey.* Adapted and illustrated by Gareth Hinds. Cambridge, MA: Candlewick Press, 2010. (MS & HS)

Kovac, Tommy. *Wonderland.* Illustrated by Sonny Liew. New York: Disney Enterprises, 2006. (MS & HS)

Lee, Tony. *Excalibur: The Legend of King Arthur.* Cambridge, MA: Candlewick Press, 2010. (MS & HS)

Melville, Herman. *Moby Dick.* Adapted by Will Eisner. NBM, 2001. (MS & HS)

Outlaw: The Legend of Robin Hood. Adapted by Tony Lee & illustrated by Sam Hart and Artur Fujita. Cambridge, MA: Candlewick Press, 2009. (MS & HS)

Rudyard, Kipling. *The Jungle Book.* Adapted by Jean-Blaise Mitildji and illustrated by TieKo. San Diego, CA: IDW Publishing, 2009. (MS)

Ray Bradbury's Fahrenheit 451: The Authorized Adaptation. Adapted and illustrated by Tim Hamilton. New York: Hill and Wang, 2009. (HS)

Sfar, Joann, Antoine de Saint-Exupéry, and Brigitte Findakly. *The Little Prince*. Boston: Houghton Mifflin Harcourt. 2010. (HS)

Shakespeare, William. *King Lear*. Adapted and illustrated by Gareth Hinds. Cambridge, MA: Candlewick Press, 2009. (MS & HS)

Shakespeare, William. *The Merchant of Venice*. Adapted and illustrated by Gareth Hinds. Cambridge, MA: Candlewick Press. 2008. (MS & HS)

Stoker, Bram. *Dracula*. Adapted and illustrated by Ben Templesmith. San Diego, CA: IDW Publishing, 2009. (MS & HS)

Suggested Titles in a Series

All Action Classics*

Dumas, Alexandre. *The Three Musketeers*. Adapted by Jim Pipe and illustrated by Penko Gelev. Graphic Classics Ser. New York: Barron's Educational Series, 2008. (MS & HS)

Homer. *The Odyssey*. Adapted Tim Mucci and illustrated by Ben Caldwell. All Action Classics Ser. New York: Sterling Publishing, 2010. (MS & HS)

Stevenson, Robert. *Kidnapped*. Adapted by Fiona MacDonald and illustrated by Penko Gelev. Graphic Classics Ser. New York: Barron's Educational Series, 2007. (MS & HS)

Stoker, Bram. *Dracula*. Adapted by Michael Mucci and illustrated by Ben Caldwell. All Action Classics Ser. New York: Sterling Publishing, 2008. (MS & HS)

Twain, Mark. *The Adventures of Huckleberry Finn*. Adapted by Tom Ratliff and illustrated by Penko Gelev. Graphic Classics Ser. New York: Barron's Educational Series, 2008. (MS & HS)

Classical Comic Series†

Bronte, Charlotte. *Jane Eyre: The Graphic Novel*. Adapted by Amy Corzine and illustrated by John Burns, et al. Towcester, UK: Classical Comics, 2009. (MS & HS)

Dickens, Charles. *A Christmas Carol: The Graphic Novel*. Adapted by Sean Wilson and illustrated by Mike Collins, et al. Towcester, UK: Classical Comics, 2008. (MS & HS)

Dickens, Charles. *Great Expectations: The Graphic Novel*. Adapted by Jen Green and illustrated by John Stokes, et al. Towcester, UK: Classical Comics, 2009. (MS & HS)

Shakespeare, William. *Macbeth: The Graphic Novel*. Adapted by John McDonald and illustrated by Jon Haward, et al. Towcester, UK: Classical Comics, 2008. (MS & HS)

Shelley, Mary. *Frankenstein: The Graphic Novel*. Adapted by Jason Cobley and illustrated by Declan Shalvey, et al. Towcester, UK: Classical Comics, 2009. (MS & HS)

Classics Illustrated Series

Carroll, Lewis. *Through the Looking Glass*. Adapted and illustrated by Kyle Baker. Classics Illustrated Ser. New York: Papercutz, 2008. (MS & HS)

Dickens, Charles. *Great Expectations*. Adapted and illustrated by Rick Geary. Classics Illustrated Ser. New York: Papercutz, 2008. (HS)

Grahame, Kenneth. *The Wind in the Willows*. Adapted and illustrated by Michel Plessix. Classics Illustrated Ser. New York: Papercutz, 2008. (MS & HS)

---

*Additional titles are available in Barron's Educational Series.
†All of these titles are available in Original Text, Plain Text and Quick Text. There are additional titles available in the Classical Comics Series.

Hawthorne, Nathaniel. *The Scarlet Letter.* Adapted by Craig Russell and illustrated by Jill Thompson. Classics Illustrated Ser. New York: Papercutz, 2009. (HS)

Tales of the Brothers Grimm. Adapted and illustrated by Mazan, Philip Petit, and Cecile Chicault. Classics Illustrated Ser. New York: Papercutz, 2008. (MS & HS)

Graphic Classics‡

Graphic Classics: Bram Stoker. Edited by Tom Pomplun. Graphic Classics Ser. Mount Horeb, MI: Eureka Productions, 2007. (HS)

Graphic Classics: Jack London. Edited by Tom Pomplun. Graphic Classics Ser. Mount Horeb, MI: Eureka Productions, 2006. (MS)

Graphic Classics: Louisa May Alcott. Edited by Tom Pomplun. Graphic Classics Ser. Mount Horeb, MI: Eureka Productions, 2009. (MS & HS)

Graphic Classics: Mark Twain. Edited by Tom Pomplun. Graphic Classics Ser. Mount Horeb, MI: Eureka Productions, 2007. (MS & HS)

Graphic Classics: O. Henry. Edited by Tom Pomplun. Graphic Classics Ser. Mounth Horeb, MI: Eureka Productions, 2005. (MS & HS)

Graphic Planet/Graphic Classics Series

Barrie, J. M. *Peter Pan.* Adapted and illustrated by Rod Espinosa. Graphic Classics Ser. Minneapolis, MN: ABDO Publishing, 2007. (MS)

London, Jack. *White Fang.* Adapted and illustrated by Joe Dunn. Graphic Classics Ser. Minneapolis, MN: ABDO Publishing, 2007. (MS)

Pyle, Howard. *Robin Hood.* Adapted and illustrated by Joe Dunn. Graphic Classics Ser. Minneapolis, MN: ABDO Publishing, 2007. (MS)

Verne, Jules. *Around the World in 80 Days.* Adapted and illustrated by Rod Espinosa. Graphic Classics Ser. Minneapolis, MN: ABDO Publishing, 2007. (MS)

Wells, H. G. *The Time Machine.* Adapted and illustrated by Joe Dunn. Graphic Classics Ser. Minneapolis, MN: ABDO Publishing, 2007. (MS)

Graphic Planet/Graphic Shakespeare Series§

Shakespeare, William. *As You Like It.* Adapted by Vincent Goodwin and illustrated by Rod Espinosa. Graphic Shakespeare Ser. Minneapolis, MN: ABDO Publishing, 2010. (MS & HS)

Shakespeare, William. *Julius Caesar.* Adapted by Vincent Goodwin and illustrated by Fred Perry. Graphic Shakespeare Ser. Minneapolis, MN: ABDO Publishing, 2010. (MS & HS)

Shakespeare, William. *King Lear.* Adapted by Brian Farrens and illustrated by Chris Allen. Graphic Shakespeare Ser. Minneapolis, MN: ABDO Publishing, 2008. (MS & HS)

Shakespeare, William. *Much Ado about Nothing.* Adapted by Vincent Goodwin and illustrated by Rod Espinosa. Graphic Shakespeare Ser. Minneapolis, MN: ABDO Publishing, 2010. (MS & HS)

Shakespeare, William. *Romeo and Juliet.* Adapted by Joeming Dunn and illustrated by Rod Espinosa. Graphic Shakespeare Ser. Minneapolis, MN: ABDO Publishing, 2008. (MS & HS)

---

‡Additional titles are available in the Graphic Classics Series.
§Additional titles are available in the Graphic Shakespeare Series.

Graphic Planet—Graphic Novel Adventures of Sherlock Holmes

Doyle, Sir Arthur. *The Adventure of Abby Grange.* Adapted by Vincent Goodwin and illustrated by Ben Dunn. Graphic Novel Adventures of Sherlock Holmes Ser. Minneapolis, MN: ABDO Publishing, 2010. (MS & HS)

Doyle, Sir Arthur. *The Adventure of the Dancing Men.* Adapted by Vincent Goodwin and illustrated by Ben Dunn. Graphic Novel Adventures of Sherlock Holmes Ser. Minneapolis, MN: ABDO Publishing, 2010. (MS & HS)

Doyle, Sir Arthur. *The Adventure of the Empty House.* Adapted by Vincent Goodwin and illustrated by Ben Dunn. Graphic Novel Adventures of Sherlock Holmes Ser. Minneapolis, MN: ABDO Publishing, 2010. (MS & HS)

Doyle, Sir Arthur. *The Adventure of the Norwood Builder.* Adapted by Vincent Goodwin and illustrated by Ben Dunn. Graphic Novel Adventures of Sherlock Holmes Ser. Minneapolis, MN: ABDO Publishing, 2010. (MS & HS)

Doyle, Sir Arthur. *The Adventure of the Red-Headed League.* Adapted by Vincent Goodwin and illustrated by Ben Dunn. Graphic Novel Adventures of Sherlock Holmes Ser. Minneapolis, MN: ABDO Publishing, 2010. (MS & HS)

Graphic Revolve Series **

Baum, Frank. *The Wizard of Oz.* Adapted by Martin Powell and illustrated by Jorge Break. Graphic Revolve Ser. Mankato, MN: Stone Arch Books, 2009. (MS)

Caroll, Lewis. *Alice in Wonderland.* Adapted by Martin Powell and illustrated by Daniel Perez. Graphic Revolve Ser. Mankato, MN: Stone Arch Books, 2009. (MS)

Collodi, Carlo. *Pinocchio.* Adapted by Martin Powell and illustrated by Alfonso Ruiz. Graphic Revolve Ser. Mankato, MN: Stone Arch Books, 2009. (MS)

Kipling, Rudyard. *The Jungle Book.* Adapted by Carl Bowen and illustrated by Gerardo Sandoval. Graphic Revolve Ser. Mankato, MN: Stone Arch Books, 2009. (MS)

Sewell, Anna. *Black Beauty.* Adapted by L. L. Owens and illustrated by Jennifer Tanner. Graphic Revolve Ser. Mankato, MN: Stone Arch Books, 2006. (MS)

Illustrated Classics Series

Dostoevsky, Fyodor. *Crime and Punishment.* Adapted by David Mairowitz and illustrated by Alain Korkos. Illustrated Classics Ser. New York: Sterling Publishing, 2009. (HS)

Doyle, Sir Arthur. *A Study in Scarlet: A Sherlock Holmes Graphic Novel.* Adapted by Ian Edginton and illustrated by I. N. J. Culbard. Illustrated Classics Ser. New York: Sterling Publishing, 2010. (MS & HS)

Poe, Edgar. *Nevermore: A Graphic Adaptation of Edgar Allan Poe's Short Stories.* Produced by Metro Media. Illustrated Classics Ser. New York: Sterling Publishing, 2008. (MS & HS)

Stevenson, Robert. *Dr. Jekyll and Mr. Hyde.* Adapted by Andrzej Klimowski and illustrated by Danusia Schejbal. Illustrated Classics Ser. New York: Sterling Publishing, 2009. (HS)

Wilde, Oscar. *The Picture of Dorian Gray.* Adapted by Ian Edginton and illustrated by I. N. J. Culbard. Illustrated Classics Ser. New York: Sterling Publishing, 2009. (HS)

**Additional titles are available in the Graphic Revolve Series. The *Graphic Revolve Series* is also available in Spanish, *Graphic Revolve en Espanol.*

Manga Shakespeare Series[††]

Shakespeare, William. *As You Like It*. Adapted by Richard Appignanesi and illustrated by Chie Kutsuwada. Manga Shakespeare Ser. London: SelfMadeHero, 2009. (MS & HS)

Shakespeare, William. *Hamlet*. Adapted by Richard Appignanesi and illustrated by Emma Vieceli. Manga Shakespeare Ser. London: SelfMadeHero, 2007. (MS & HS)

Shakespeare, William. *Julius Caesar*. Adapted by Richard Appignanesi and illustrated by Mustashrik. Manga Shakespeare Ser. London: SelfMadeHero, 2008. (MS & HS)

Shakespeare, William. *Macbeth*. Adapted by Richard Appignanesi and illustrated by Robert Deas. Manga Shakespeare Ser. London: SelfMadeHero, 2008. (MS & HS)

Shakespeare, William. *A Midsummer Night's Dream*. Adapted by Richard Appignanesi and illustrated by Kate Brown. Manga Shakespeare Ser. London: SelfMadeHero, 2008. (MS & HS)

Marvel Illustrated Classics[‡‡]

Austen, Jane. *Pride and Prejudice*. Adapted by Nancy Butler & illustrated by Hugo Petrus. New York: Marvel Books, 2009. (HS)

Baum, Frank. *The Wonderful Wizard of Oz*. Adapted by Eric Shanower and illustrated by Skottie Young. New York: Marvel Books, 2009. (MS & HS)

Cooper, James. *The Last of the Mohicans*. Adapted by Roy Thomas and illustrated by Steve Kurth and Denis Medri. New York: Marvel Books, 2008. (HS)

Dumas, Alexandre. *The Three Musketeers*. Adapted by Roy Thomas and illustrated by Hugo Petrus. New York: Marvel Books, 2009. (HS)

Stevenson, Robert. *Treasure Island*. Adapted by Roy Thomas and illustrated by Mario Gully. New York: Marvel Books, 2009. (MS & HS)

No Fear Shakespeare Series[§§]

Shakespeare, William. *Antony and Cleopatra*. Adapted by John Crowther. New York: Spark Notes, 2006. (HS) Shakespeare, William. *As You Like It*. Adapted by John Crowther. New York: Spark Notes, 2004. (HS)

Shakespeare, William. *Hamlet*. Adapted by John Crowther. New York: Spark Notes, 2003. (HS)

Shakespeare, William. *Henry V*. Adapted by John Crowther. New York: Spark Notes, 2005. (HS)

Shakespeare, William. *Julius Caesar*. Adapted by John Crowther. New York: Spark Notes, 2003. (HS)

Puffin Graphics Series

Baum, Frank. *Wizard of Oz: The Graphic Novel*. Adapted and illustrated by Michael Cavallaro. Puffin Graphics Ser. New York: Penguin, 2005. (MS & HS)

Crane, Stephen. *Red Badge of Courage: The Graphic Novel*. Adapted and illustrated by Wayne Vansant. Puffin Graphics Ser. New York: Penguin, 2005. (MS & HS)

Sewell, Anna. *Black Beauty: The Graphic Novel*. Adapted and illustrated by June Brigman. Puffin Graphics Ser. New York: Penguin, 2005. (MS & HS)

[††]Additional titles are available in the Manga Shakespeare Series.
[‡‡]Additional titles are available in the Marvel Illustrated Classic Series.
[§§]Additional titles are available in the No Fear Shakespeare Series.

Shelley, Mary. *Frankenstein: The Graphic Novel*. Adapted by Gary Reed and illustrated by Frazer Irving. Puffin Graphics Ser. New York: Penguin, 2005. (MS & HS)

Stevenson, Robert. *Treasure Island: The Graphic Novel*. Adapted and illustrated by Tim Hamilton. Puffin Graphics Ser. New York: Penguin, 2005. (MS & HS)

Saddlebacks' Illustrated Classics***

London, Jack. *The Call of the Wild*. Irvine, CA: Saddleback Educational Pub., 2006. (MS & HS)

Shakespeare, William. *Romeo and Juliet*. Irvine, CA: Saddleback Educational Pub., 2006. (MS & HS)

Shakespeare, William. *A Tale of Two Cities*. Irvine, CA: Saddleback Educational Pub., (2006). (MS & HS)

Verne, Jules. *Journey to the Center of the Earth*. Irvine, CA: Saddleback, 2006. (MS & HS)

Wyss, Johann David. *The Swiss Family Robinson*. Irvine, CA: Saddleback Pub., 2006 (MS & HS)

Lesson Plans

Lesson Plan Title: *The Raven* by Edgar Allan Poe

Grade Level: MS

Subject Area: English Language Arts

Curriculum Focus/Concepts: Literature, Edgar Allan Poe, poetry, literary devices

Graphic Novel Tie-In:

The works of Edgar Allan Poe have both fascinated and terrified middle and high school students for years. A unit on his poem, *The Raven*, is a popular mainstay in the English Language Arts curriculum. Poe's most famous poem has been portrayed visually for decades, from a movie starring Vincent Price to an episode of *The Simpsons*. Now, graphic novels can visually bring *The Raven*, and other of Poe's works, to life for a new generation of learners. The two titles listed below showcase *The Raven*, as well as some of Poe's other poems and stories.

The Raven and Other Poems, illustrated by Gahan Wilson, includes nine graphic adaptations of some of Poe's darkest poems, including *The Raven*. The eeriness of the poems is enhanced by the artist's use of pastels and ink.

Nevermore: A Graphic Adaptation of Edgar Allan Poe's Short Stories features *The Raven* and eight other works illustrated by top comic artists. Historical context precedes each of the pieces, and there is a biographical segment about Poe at the end of the book.

Objectives:

Students will learn about the life of Edgar Allan Poe.

Students will explore connections between the life and writings of Edgar Allan Poe.

Students will listen to a reading of *The Raven* and analyze it.

***Additional titles are available in the No Fear Shakespeare Series.

Students will compare and contrast versions of the poem, *The Raven*.
Students will examine literary devices in the poem and learn new vocabulary.

Materials/Resources:
Books
Poe, Edgar. *The Raven and Other Poems*. Adapted and illustrated by Gahan Wilson. Classics Illustrated Ser. New York: Papercutz, 2009.
Poe, Edgar. *Nevermore: A Graphic Adaptation of Edgar Allan Poe's Short Stories*. Produced by Metro Media. Illustrated Classics Ser. New York: Sterling Publishing, 2008.
Poe, Edgar Allan, and Ryan Price. *The Raven*. Visions in poetry. Toronto, ON: KCP Poetry. 2006.

Websites
Knowing Poe http://knowingpoe.thinkport.org/default_flash.asp
The Interactive Raven—Teacher's First Website http://www.teachersfirst.com/share/raven
The Raven—Background about the poem by NPR www.npr.org/programs/morning/features/patc/raven

Procedures/Activities:
Begin the lesson with an introduction to Edgar Allan Poe.
Read the poem, *The Raven*, or play a recorded version of it.
Show students the *Interactive Raven* website to examine literary devices and vocabulary in the poem.
Project, or share two graphic novel versions of *The Raven*.
Have students work in pairs to compare and contrast the versions of the poem they examined in class.

Discussion Questions:
What does the raven symbolize?
What is the setting of the poem, and how does it contribute to the mood of the poem?
What aspects of Poe's life influenced his writings?
How does the artwork in the graphic novel reflect its topic?
How does each artist's medium and style make the art interdependent with the text?

Closure:
When the pairs finish discussing the poem, have them come together and tell the class which version was their favorite and why.

Extension Activities:
Have students compare and contrast some of Poe's other poems and/or short stories in the form of an oral or written report.
Have students read the novel, *The Man Who Was Poe*, a fictional account of Poe's life by Avi.

Assessment:
Assess students on activities conducted in class and their participation with their classmates.

Lesson Plan Title: *Thus, With a Kiss I Die*: Analyzing the Romeo and Juliet Death Scene

Grade Level: HS

Subject Area: English Language Arts

Curriculum Focus/Concepts: Literature, William Shakespeare, plays, Elizabethan period, Elizabethan language

Graphic Novel Tie-In:
   Although movies about Romeo and Juliet are typically popular with adolescents, students often struggle when reading the original text. In particular, they have difficulty understanding the poetic language, context, and cultural details found in the Shakespearean play. The Elizabethan language and vocabulary is noticeably different from what they experience in their daily lives. Graphic novels can help to demystify the complexity of the play's language by presenting it in a variety of versions, and with graphics that support the text. Allowing students to use the graphic novel versions of *Romeo and Juliet* can help provide an excellent introduction to Shakespearean drama.

Objectives:
Students will learn about the final death scene in the play, *Romeo and Juliet*.
Students will understand the scene's original Shakespearean text by comparing and contrasting graphic novel adaptations.
Students will learn about the Elizabethan period and the language of the time.
Students will work collaboratively to write their own versions of the death scenes, using modern day English.

Materials/Resources:
Books
Romeo and Juliet: The Graphic Novel, Original Text. Adapted by Jon McDonald and illustrated by Will Volley, et al. Towcester, UK: Classical Comics, 2009.
Romeo and Juliet: The Graphic Novel, Plain Text. Adapted by Jon McDonald and illustrated by Will Volley, et al. Towcester, UK: Classical Comics, 2009.
Romeo and Juliet: The Graphic Novel, Quick Text. Adapted by Jon McDonald and illustrated by Will Volley, et al. Towcester, UK: Classical Comics, 2009.
Romeo and Juliet. Adapted by Richard Appignanesi and illustrated by Sonia Leong. Manga Shakespeare Ser. London: SelfMadeHero, 2007.
Romeo and Juliet. Adapted by Joeming Dunn and illustrated by Rod Espinosa. Graphic Shakespeare Ser. Minneapolis, MN: ABDO Publishing, 2008.
Romeo and Juliet: No Fear Shakespeare. Adapted by John Crowther. No Fear Shakespeare Ser. Toronto, Ontario: Spark Publishing, 2008.
Chrisp, Peter, and Steve Teague. 2002. *Shakespeare.* Eyewitness Guides. New York: DK Pub.
Claybourne, Anna, Rebecca Treays, and Felicity Brooks. 1997. *The World of Shakespeare.* Tulsa, Okla: EDC Pub

Websites
Mr. William Shakespeare http://shakespeare.palomar.edu/Default.htm
Folger Shakespeare Library http://www.folger.edu/index.cfm

Procedures/Activities:
Begin the lesson with an introduction to William Shakespeare.
Provide an overview of the play, *Romeo and Juliet*.
Use books and websites to help you depict the Elizabethan period and language.
Project, or share one of the graphic novel versions of the death scenes of both Romeo and Juliet. (There are a variety of graphic novel versions that can be used to differentiate instruction for your students.)
Break the students into groups. Give each group 1–2 of the graphic novel adaptations of *Romeo and Juliet*.
Provide each group with a handout of the original Shakespearean text versions of the two death scenes.
Have the students write their own versions of the death scenes, using modern-day English.

Discussion Questions:
What could have been done to prevent Romeo and Juliet's deaths from occurring?
What good, if any, has come from their deaths?
What are some ways that language has changed since the Elizabethan period?
How does the artwork in the graphic novels reflect its topic?
How does each artist's medium and style make the art interdependent with the text?

Closure:
When the groups are finished, have them come together and share their group's versions with the class.

Extension Activities:
Have students work in groups to write a modern-day newspaper article based on the tragic deaths of Romeo and Juliet. See the following example from the BBC's, *60 Second Star*: www.bbc.co.uk/print/drama/shakespeare/60secondshakespeare/themes _romeojuliet.shtml

Assessment:
Assess students on their group projects and participation in their groups.

Chapter 11

Legendary Resources: Traditional Literature in Graphic Novels

Introduction

Traditional literature is a genre in which the literature was passed down orally from one generation to the next. The subgenres of traditional literature include mythology, fables, legends, folk and fairy tales, tall tales, pourquoi tales, trickster tales, and more. When today's students read traditional literature, it enables them to develop an understanding and appreciation for the customs, superstitions, and beliefs of previous cultures. When traditional literature is presented in the graphic novel format, it can make the content more user-friendly to today's increasingly visual generation of students. For example, *The Lightning Thief, the Graphic Novel* (Riordan, 2010), along with the original book and movie, has sparked an interest in mythology among middle school students. Providing alternative retellings of traditional literature in schools may engage students who might not otherwise be interested in reading this genre. There are a growing number of graphic novels that are adaptations of traditional literature. The titles presented in the lists below are well-told and re-created in an imaginative way. Using these engaging and readable titles with your students offers them a new literary experience with some enduring myths and legends.

Connecting to the Standards

AASL Standards for the 21st-Century Learner

4.1.1 Read, view, and listen for pleasure and personal growth.

4.1.3 Respond to literature and creative expressions of ideas in various formats and genres.

The Bottom Line

Middle and high school students will enjoy seeing traditional literature in a new light when you share graphic novel adaptations with them.

NCTE/IRA Standard for English Language Arts

Standard 3 Students apply a wide range of strategies to comprehend, interpret, evaluate, and appreciate texts. They draw on their prior experience, their interactions with other readers and writers, their knowledge of word meaning and of other texts, their word identification strategies, and their understanding of textual features (e.g., sound-letter correspondence, sentence structure, context, graphics).

Comic Connections

Children of all ages enjoy listening to a good fairy tale, especially ones that are beautifully illustrated. Use a document camera, as you read aloud some of Oscar Wilde's fairy tales from the graphic novel series illustrated by Russell P. Craig. After they have heard some of Wilde's fairy tales, ask the students to select their favorite and explain why they chose it.

Suggested Titles by Middle and High School (MS & HS)

Dembicki, Matt. *Trickster: Native American Tales: A Graphic Collection*. Golden, CO: Fulcrum Pub., 2010. (MS & HS)

Foley, Ryan. Illustrated by Sankha Banerjee. *Stolen Hearts: The Love of Eros and Psyche*, New Delhi: India, 2011. (MS)

Hale, Shannon, Dean Hale, and Nathan Hale. *Calamity Jack*. New York: Bloomsbury. 2010. (MS)

Hale, Shannon, Dean Hale, and Nathan Hale. *Rapunzel's Revenge*. New York: Bloomsbury, 2008. (MS)

Homer. *The Odyssey*. Adapted and illustrated by Gareth Hinds. Cambridge, MA: Candlewick Press, 2010. (MS & HS)

Homer. *The Odyssey*. Adapted by Michael Mucci and illustrated by Ben Caldwell. All Action Classics Ser. New York: Sterling Publishing, 2010. (MS & HS)

Medley, Linda, Jane Yolen, Gary Groth, Adam Grano, and Todd Klein. *Castle Waiting*. Seattle, WA: Fantagraphics, 2006. (MS & HS)

O'Connor, George. *Athena: Grey-Eyed Goddess*. New York: First Second, 2010. (MS)

O'Connor, George. *Zeus: King of the Gods*. New York: First Second, 2010. (MS)

Suggested Titles in a Series

Age of Bronze

Shanower, Eric. *A Thousand Ships*. Age of Bronze ser., Orange, CA: Image Comics, 2001.

Shanower, Eric. *Sacrifice*. Age of Bronze ser., Orange, CA: Image Comics, 2005.

Shanower, Eric. *Betrayal—Part One*. Age of Bronze ser., Orange, CA: Image Comics, 2007.

Fairy Tales of Oscar Wilde

Wilde, Oscar. *The Fairy Tales of Oscar Wilde*, Volume 1. Illustrated by Russell P. Craig. New York: Nantier, Beall, Minoustchine (NBM), 1992.

Wilde, Oscar. *The Fairy Tales of Oscar Wilde*, Volume 2. Illustrated by Russell P. Craig. New York: Nantier, Beall, Minoustchine (NBM), 1996.

Wilde, Oscar. *The Fairy Tales of Oscar Wilde*, Volume 3. Illustrated by Russell P. Craig. New York: Nantier, Beall, Minoustchine (NBM), 1998.

Wilde, Oscar. *The Fairy Tales of Oscar Wilde*, Volume 4. Illustrated by Russell P. Craig. New York: Nantier, Beall, Minoustchine (NBM), 2004.

Graphic Mythology

Jeffrey, Gary. *African Myths*. *Graphic Mythology*. New York: Rosen Pub. Group, 2006.

Jeffrey, Gary, and Romano Felmang. *Egyptian Myths*. Graphic Mythology. New York: Rosen Pub. Group, 2006.

Shone, Rob. *Greek Myths*. Graphic Mythology. New York: Rosen Pub. Group, 2006.

Shone, Rob, and Claudia Saraceni. *Chinese Myths*. Graphic Mythology. New York: Rosen Pub. Group, 2006.

West, David Alexander, and Ross Watton. *Roman Myths*. Graphic Mythology. New York: Rosen Pub. Group, 2005.

Graphic Myths and Legend Series[*]

Croall, Marie P., and Clint Hilinski. *Sinbad: Sailing into Peril: an Arabian Tale*. Minneapolis, MN: Graphic Universe, 2008.

Fontes, Justine; Fontes, Ron; and Kurth, Steve. *Demeter & Persephone: Spring Held Hostage: A Greek Myth*. Minneapolis, MN: Graphic Universe, 2007.

Jolley, Dan, Ron Randall, and Guanzhong Luo. *Guan Yu: Blood Brothers to the End: A Chinese Legend*. Minneapolis, MN: Graphic Universe, 2008.

Limke, Jeff, and John McCrea. *Theseus: Battling the Minotaur*. Minneapolis, MN: Graphic Universe, 2008.

Limke, Jeff, Thomas Yeates, and Thomas Malory. *Arthur & Lancelot: The Fight for Camelot, an English Legend*. Minneapolis, MN: Graphic Universe, 2008.

Storrie, Paul D., Steve Kurth, and Barbara Schulz. *Hercules: The Twelve Labors*. Graphic myths and legends. Minneapolis, MN: Graphic Universe, 2007.

Graphic Revolve Series[†]

Hall, Margaret, and Christopher Richards. *King Arthur and the Knights of the Round Table*. Minneapolis, MN: Stone Arch Books, 2007.

Hoena, B. A., Tod Smith, and Washington Irving. *The Legend of Sleepy Hollow*. Minneapolis, MN: Stone Arch Books, 2008.

Powell, Martin, and José Alfonso Ocampo Ruiz. *The Adventures of Hercules*. Minneapolis, MN: Stone Arch Books, 2009.

Yomtov, Nelson, and Gerardo Sandoval. *Jason and the Golden Fleece*. Minneapolis, MN: Stone Arch Books. 2009.

Yomtov, Nelson, and Tod Smith. *Theseus and the Minotaur*. Minneapolis, MN: Stone Arch Books, 2009.

---

[*]Additional titles are available in the Graphic Universe Series.
[†]Additional titles are available in the Graphic Revolve Series.

Lesson Plans

Lesson Plan Title: A "Myth-ing" Person's Alphabet Book

Grade Level: MS

Subject Areas: English Language Arts, Social Studies, Art

Curriculum Focus/Concepts: Traditional Literature, Mythology, Greek gods and goddesses

Graphic Novel Tie-Ins:

Thanks to the enormous popularity of the Percy Jackson and the Olympian series by Rick Riordan, there is a renewed interest in mythology by middle school students. Graphic novels about mythology complement the Percy Jackson series, as well as other mythology books in your collection. For example, *Zeus: King of the Gods* (O'Connor, 2010) is an award-winning graphic novel that will engage students who have never read about Zeus, as well as those who want to learn more about the king of the gods. *Athena: Grey-Eyed Goddess* (O'Connor, 2010) is the second in the Olympians series, which will be followed by ten other titles from First Second Books. The lists below offer suggestions for other graphic novel adaptations of graphic novels that you can share with students when they want to learn more about mythology.

Objectives:
Students will learn about the elements of Greek mythology.
Students will demonstrate an understanding of the Greek gods and goddesses.
Students will work collaboratively to research Greek gods and goddesses.
Students will create a "Myth-ing" Persons graphic novel alphabet book for the class.

Materials/Resources:
Books
D'Aulaire, Ingri. *Book of Greek Myths*, New York: Delacorte Books for Young Readers.
Evslin, Bernard. *Heroes, Gods, and Monsters of the Greek Myths*, New York: Laurel Leaf
Fontes, Justine; Fontes, Ron. Illustrated byKurth, Steve, *Demeter & Persephone: Spring Held Hostage: A Greek Myth. Minneapolis*, MN: Graphic Universe, 2007.
Hamilton, Edith W. *Mythology*, New York: Little Brown, 1942.
O'Connor, George. *Athena: Grey-Eyed Goddess*. New York: First Second, 2010.
O'Connor, George. *Zeus: King of the Gods*. New York: First Second, 2010. (MS)
Shone, Rob. *Greek Myths. Graphic Mythology*. New York: Rosen Pub. Group, 2006.
Storrie, Paul D., Steve Kurth, and Barbara Schulz. *Hercules: The Twelve Labors. Graphic Myths and Legends*. Minneapolis, MN: Graphic Universe, 2007.

Websites
Ancient Greece http://www.ancientgreece.com/s/Main_Page
Encyclopedia of Greek Mythology http://www.mythweb.com/encyc/index.html

Encyclopedia Mythica—Greek mythology http://www.pantheon.org/areas/mythology/europe/greek/

Mythweb http://us.macmillan.com/CMS400/uploadedFiles/FirstSecond/Menu_Items/9781596434325TG.pdf

Materials:
Paper, pencils, markers, colored pencils, and crayons

Procedure/Activities:
Begin the lesson with an introduction to Greek mythology.
Project or share some of the stories in *Zeus* and/or *Athena* by George O'Connor.

Discussion Questions:
What are the names of other gods and goddesses that you know about?
What are some of the characteristics of the gods and goddesses you learned about?
Can you think of any products, cars, and so on named after gods and goddesses? (Possibilities include Trident gum, Ajax cleaner, and Hermes ties.)
Break the students into groups. Divide up the letters of the alphabet so that each group has several letters.
Have students create pages for a graphic novel alphabet book. They should create one page about a god or goddess for each letter that their group is assigned. They will draw a graphic novel rendition of each god and goddess they select, and write 4–5 sentences about them on the same page.
Provide the groups with access to books and computers to research the gods and goddesses.
Allow students time to research, select the gods and goddesses for their letters, and create their pages.

Closure:
When the groups are finished creating their gods' and goddesses' pages, have them come together and share them with the class. Once all of the ABC sheets are complete, bind them into a "Myth-ing" Persons Graphic Novel ABC Book.

Extension Activities:
Have students read *The Lightning Thief* (2005), the first book in the Percy Jackson and the Olympians series by Rick Riordan. Put students in literature circles. Ask students to discuss the book, and locate references to gods and goddesses that they have learned about. Have students compare the characteristics they found in their research with the way the gods or goddesses are portrayed in Riordan's book. Have students make lists of similar and contrasting characteristics to present to the class.
*If there is not enough time for the students to read the original version of *The Lightning Thief*, share parts of the graphic novel version with them and have a similar class discussion.
Percy Jackson and the Olympians: The Lightning Thief Graphic Novel by Rick Riordan (Hyperion Books, 2010).

Assessment:
Assess the students through the use of rubrics, on their ABC book pages, and partici-pation in their literature circles.

Lesson Plan Title: Native American Trickster Tales

Grade Level: HS

Subject Area: English Language Arts

Curriculum Focus/Concepts: Traditional literature, folklore, Native American Indians

Graphic Novel Tie-In:
   Trickster: Native American Tales: A Graphic Collection by Matt Dembicki (Fulcrum, 2010). Includes over twenty trickster stories, in graphic novel format, from various Native American traditions, including tales about coyotes, rabbits, ravens, and other crafty creatures and their mischievous activities.

Objectives:
Students will recognize and understand the elements of Native American trickster tales.
Students will compare and contrast themes of several Native American trickster tales.
Students will identify human traits associated with particular animals in Native American trickster stories.
Students will describe the ways in which animals in Native American trickster tales are used to point out human strengths and weaknesses.

Materials/Resources:
Books
Bruchach, Joseph. *The Girl Who Helped Thunder and Other Native American Folktales*, New York: Sterling, 2008. (Contains two trickster tales, How Rabbit Got Wisdom and How Raven Brought Back the Sun.)
Datlow, Ellen and Windlin, Terri. Illustrations by Charles Vess. *The Coyote Road: Trickster Tales*, New York: Viking, 2007.
Dembicki, Matt. *Trickster: Native American Tales*, Golden, CO: Fulcrum, 2010.

Websites
American Folklore—Native American Myths http://americanfolklore.net/folklore/native-american-myths
Additional titles or websites that include Native American trickster tales.

Procedure/Activities:
Provide the students with background information on Native American trickster tales.

Project, or share, 2–3 trickster tales in the graphic novel, *Trickster, Native American Tales*.

- Have students briefly discuss each tale after you present it to them.
- Ask the students to discuss the layout, color, and so on of the pictures, and whether or not the pictures helped them understand the story.

Break the students into groups. Provide each group with a different trickster tale from other sources (two possible titles are listed above). Have them read the tale aloud in their groups.

In their groups, students should discuss the following:

Discussion Questions:
How would you compare the tale you read in your group with the graphic novel tales that the teacher shared with you?
Which format did you like better, the graphic novel version or the text-only version? Why?
What are some of the human characteristics of the animals in the trickster tales you examined today?
What are some examples of the ways in which the animals characterized human strengths and weaknesses?

Closure:
Have groups present an overview of their discussion to the rest of the class. As a class, summarize any common themes that were presented.

Extension Activities:
Native language can be used in powerful ways by different cultures. For example, the language used in the trickster tales can help people understand Native American culture. Tell students that Native American language played an important role in World War II. Show them the following website about Code Talkers, from the National Museum of the American Indian in Washington, DC. http://www.nmai.si.edu/education/codetalkers/. Allow students time to explore the website to learn more about Code Talkers. Suggest that students interested in learning more should read the book, *Code Talkers*, by Joseph Bruchac (Dial, 2005).

Assessment:
Assess students on their content knowledge and group participation.

Chapter 12

Biographies and Autobiographies: Memoirs, Manga, and More

Introductions

Biographies introduce readers to heroes, presidents, rock stars, athletes, scientists, and more. Biographies can also personalize history for readers by presenting true stories of life, murder, and war. For example, *Maus: A Survivor's Tale* (Spielgeman, 1987) is a Pulitzer Prize–winning memoir of the author's father, a Polish Jew and Holocaust survivor. In addition to helping students understand history, biographies can help them understand what motivates famous people. Reading graphic novel biographies can help students identify with the person about whom the graphic novel is written. The illustrations in graphic novels add realism to the person's life, at the same time it engages adolescent readers.

Connecting to the Standards

AAS Standards for the 21st-Century Learner

4.1.2 Read widely and fluently to make connections with self, the world, and previous reading.

4.1.3 Respond to literature and creative expressions of ideas in various formats and genres.

NCTE/IRA Standard for English Language Arts

Standard 3 Students apply a wide range of strategies to comprehend, interpret, evaluate, and appreciate texts. They draw on their prior experience, their interactions with other readers and writers, their knowledge of word meaning and of other texts, their word identification strategies, and their understanding of textual features (e.g., sound-letter correspondence, sentence structure, context, graphics).

The Bottom Line

Graphic novels can breathe new life into familiar historical figures and introduce readers to new ones.

Comic Connections

- The Center for Cartoon Studies, along with Jump at the Sun (Hyperion Books for Children/ Disney Book Group) has published several award-winning graphic novel biographies. These include Satchel Paige, Thoreau, Houdini, and Amelia Earhart (titles listed below). You can use the following discussion guides with your students and patrons:

    Satchel Paige—http://a.dolimg.com/explore/PMPages/DCOM/books/catalog/Printable/Satchel-Paige.pdf

    Houdini—http://a.dolimg.com/explore/PMPages/DCOM/books/catalog/Printable/Houdini.pdf

    Thoreau—http://a.dolimg.com/explore/PMPages/DCOM/books/catalog/Printable/Thoreau-at-Walden.pdf

- After students finish reading a graphic novel, ask them if they would like to learn more about the illustrator of the book. If so, they can use the following encyclopedia and books to read about their graphic novel illustrator:

    Pendergast, Tom, and Sara Pendergast. *UXL Graphic Novelists: Profiles of Cutting Edge Authors and Illustrators*. Farmington Hills, MI: UXL Publishing, 2006. 3 vols. (MS & HS)

    The Library of Graphic Novelists. New York: Rosen Publishing Group, Inc. (Current titles include Art Spiegelman, Colleen Doran, Neil Gaiman, Joe Sacco, and Bryan Talbot.)

Suggested Titles by Middle and High Schools (MS & HS)

Anderson, Ho Che. *King: A Comics Biography of Martin Luther King, Jr.* Seattle, WA: Fantagraphics, 2005. (HS)

Burleigh, Robert. *Amelia Earhart Free in the Skies*. Illustrated by Bill Wylie. Boston, MA: Silver Whistle, 2003. (MS)

Burleigh, Robert. *Into the Air: The Story of the Wright Brothers' First Flight*. Illustrated by Bill Wylie. Boston, MA: Harcourt, 2002. (MS)

Colbert, C. C. *Booth*. Illustrated by Tanitoc. New York: First Second Publishing, 2010. (HS)

Dawson, Mike. *Freddie and Me: A Coming-of-Age (Bohemian) Rhapsody*. New York: Bloomsbury USA Publishing, 2008. (HS)

Geary, Rick. *J. Edgar Hoover: A Graphic Biography*. New York: Hill and Wang Publishing, 2008. (HS)

Geary, Rick. *Trotsky: A Graphic Biography*. Illustrated by Rick Geary. New York: Hill and Wang Publishing, 2009. (HS)

Guibert, Emmanuel. *The Photographer: Into War-torn Afghanistan with Doctors Without Borders*. New York: First Second Publishing, 2009. (HS)

Helfer, Andrew, and Randy DuBurke. *Malcolm X: A Graphic Biography.* New York: Hill and Wang, 2006. (HS)

Helfer, Andrew. *Ronald Reagan: A Graphic Biography.* Illustrated by Steve Buccellato and Joe Staton. New York: Hill and Wang Publishing, 2007. (HS)

Jacobson, Sid, and Ernie Colon. *Anne Frank: The Anne Frank House Authorized Graphic Biography.* New York: Hill and Want Publishing, 2010. (MS & HS)

Jones, Sabrina. *Isadora Duncan: A Graphic Biography.* New York: Hill and Wang Publishing, 2008. (HS)

O'Connor, George. *Journey into Mohawk County.* New York: First Second Publishing, 2006. (HS)

Ottaviani, Jim. *Fallout: J. Robert Oppenheimer, Leo Szilard, and the Political Science of the Atomic Bomb.* Ann Arbor, MI: G.T. Labs, 2001. (HS)

Ottaviani, Jim. *Dignifying Science: Stories about Women Scientists.* Ann Arbor, MI: G.T. Labs, 2009. (HS)

Ottaviani, Jim. *Two Fisted Science: Stories about Scientists.* Ann Arbor, MI: G.T. Labs, 2009. (HS)

Ottaviani, Jim. *Bone Sharps, Cowboys, and Thunder Lizards: A Tale of Edward Drinker Cope, Othniel Charles Marsh, and the Gilded Age of Paleontology: Stories about Scientists.* Ann Arbor, MI: G.T. Labs, 2005. (HS)

Ottaviani, Jim. *Suspended in Language: Niels Bohr's Life, Discoveries, and the Century He Shaped.* Ann Arbor, MI: G.T. Labs, 2009. (HS)

Ottaviani, Jim. *Levitation: Physics and Psychology in the Face of Deception.* Ann Arbor, MI: G.T. Labs, 2007. (HS)

Ottaviani, Jim. *Wire Mothers: Harry Harlow and the Science of Love.* Ann Arbor, MI: G.T. Labs, 2007. (HS)

Pekar, Harvey, Ed Piskor, and Paul Buhle. *The Beats: A Graphic History.* New York: Hill and Wang, 2009. (HS)

Porcellino, John. *Thoreau at Walden.* New York: Hyperion Books, 2008. (MS & HS)

Satrapi, Marjane. *Persepolis.* New York: Pantheon Books, 2003. (MS & HS)

Satrapi, Marjane. *Persepolis 2: The Story of a Return.* New York: Pantheon Books, 2004. (MS & HS)

Siegel, Siena Cherson. *To Dance: A Ballerina's Graphic Novel.* Illustrated by Mark Siegel. New York: Atheneum Books, 2006. (MS)

Spiegelman, Art. *Maus: A Survivor's Tale.* New York: Pantheon Books, 1986. (HS)

Sturm, James. *Satchel Paige: Striking Out Jim Crow.* Illustrated by Rich Tommaso. New York: Hyperion Books, 2007. (MS & HS)

Taylor, Sarah, and James Sturn. *Amelia Earhart: This Broad Ocean.* Illustrated by Bew Towle. New York: Hyperion Books, 2010. (MS & HS)

Thompson, Craig. *Blankets.* Portland, OR: Top Shelf Productions, 2003. (HS)

Suggested Titles in a Series

American Graphic Series[*]

Biskup, Agnieszka. *Houdini.* Illustrated by Pat Kinsella. American Graphic Ser. Mankato, MN: Capstone Press, 2011. (MS)

Collins, Terry. *Elvis.* Illustrated by Michele Melcher. American Graphic Ser. Mankato, MN: Capstone Press, 2011. (MS)

Collins, Terry. *Robert E. Lee.* Illustrated by Cristian Mallea. American Graphic Ser. Mankato, MN: Capstone Press, 2011. (MS)

---

[*]Additional titles are available in the American Graphic Series.

Gunderson, Jessica. *X: A Biography of Malcolm X*. Illustrated by Seitu Hayden. American Graphic Ser. Mankato, MN: Capstone Press, 2011. (MS)

Yomtov, Nel. *The Bambino*. Illustrated by Tim Foley. American Graphic Ser. Mankato, MN: Capstone Press, 2011. (MS)

Graphic Biographies Series[†]

Braun, Eric. *Booker T. Washington*. Illustrated by Cynthia Martin. Graphic Biographies Ser. Mankato, MN: Capstone Press, 2006. (MS)

Burgan, Michael. *Benedict Arnold*. Illustrated by Terry Beatty. Graphic Biographies Ser. Mankato, MN: Capstone Press, 2007. (MS)

Lassieur, Allison. *Clara Barton*. Illustrated by Brian Bascle. Graphic Biographies Ser. Mankato, MN: Capstone Press, 2006. (MS)

Robbins, Trina. *Florence Nightingale*. Illustrated by Anne Timmons. Graphic Biographies Ser. Mankato, MN: Capstone Press, 2007. (MS)

Wade, Mary Dodson. *Christopher Columbus*. Illustrated by Rod Whigham. Graphic Biographies Ser. Mankato, MN: Capstone Press, 2007. (MS)

Graphic Biographies Series[‡]

Hudson-Goff, Elizabeth, and Jonatha Brown. *Anne Frank*. Illustrated by Guus Floor, D. McHargue, and Jonathan Timmons. Graphic Biographies Ser. New York: Gareth Publishing, 2005. (MS)

O'Hern, Kerri, and Gini Holland. *Louis Armstrong*. Illustrated by Alex Campbell. Graphic Biographies Ser. New York: Gareth Publishing, 2005. (MS)

O'Hern, Kerri, and Gini Holland. *Nelson Mandela*. Illustrated by D. McHargue. Graphic Biographies Ser. New York: Gareth Publishing, 2005. (MS)

O'Hern, Kerri, and Gretchen Will Mayo. *The Wright Brothers*. Illustrated by Rebekah Isaacs and Jonathan Timmons. Graphic Biographies Ser. New York: Gareth Publishing, 2005. (MS)

O'Hern, Kerri, and Lucia Raatma. *Jackie Robinson*. Illustrated by Alex Campbell and Anthony Spay. Graphic Biographies Ser. New York: Gareth Publishing, 2005. (MS)

Graphic Biography Series[§]

Babe Ruth. Irvine, CA: Saddleback Educational Pub., 2008. (MS & HS)

Barack Obama. Irvine, CA: Saddleback Educational Pub., 2008. (MS & HS)

Marie Curie. Irvine, CA: Saddleback Educational Pub., 2008. (MS & HS)

Martin Luther King. Irvine, CA: Saddleback Educational Pub., 2008. (MS & HS)

Walt Disney. Irvine, CA: Saddleback Educational Pub., 2008. (MS & HS)

EduManga Series

Himuro, Isao. *Edu-Manga: Albert Einstein*. Illustrated by Kotaro Iwasaki. DMP Educational Ser. Gardena, CA: Digital Manga Publishing, 2006. (MS)

Kanda, Takayuki. *Edu-Manga: Ludwig Van Beethoven*. Illustrated by Naoko Takase. DMP Educational Ser. Gardena, CA: Digital Manga Publishing, 2006. (MS)

[†]Additional titles are available in the Graphic Biographies Series.
[‡]Additional titles are available in the Graphic Biographies Series.
[§]Additional titles are available in the Graphic Biography Series.

Kikai, Masahide. *Edu-Manga: Mother Teresa*. Illustrated by Ren Kishida. DMP Educational Ser. Garden, CA: Digital Manga Publishing, 2007. (MS)

Suzuki, Etsuo. *Edu-Manga: Anne Frank*. Illustrated by Yoko Miyawaki. DMP Educational Ser. Gardena, CA: Digital Manga Publishing, 2006. (MS)

Yanagawa, Sozo. *Edu-Manga: Helen Adams Keller*. Illustrated by Rie Yagi. DMP Educational Ser. Gardena, CA: Digital Manga Publishing, 2005. (MS)

Graphic Nonfiction Biographies[**]

Jeffrey, Gary. *Cleopatra: The Life of an Egyptian Queen*. Illustrated by Ross Watton. Graphic Nonfiction Ser. New York: Rosen Publishing, 2005. (MS)

Jeffrey, Gary, and Kate Petty. *Abraham Lincoln: The Life of America's Sixteenth President*. Illustrated by Mike Lacey. Graphic Nonfiction Ser. New York: Rosen Publishing, 2005. (MS)

Jeffrey, Gary, and Kate Perry. *Sitting Bull: The Life of a Lakota Sioux Chief*. Illustrated by Terry Riley. Graphic Nonfiction Ser. New York: Rosen Publishing, 2005. (MS)

Shone, Rob, and Anita Ganeri. *Alexander the Great: The Life of a King and Conqueror*. Illustrated by Chris Odgers. Graphic Nonfiction Ser. New York: Rosen Publishing, 2005. (MS)

Shone, Rob, and Anita Ganeri. *Harriet Tubman: The Life of an African-American*. Graphic Nonfiction Ser. New York: Rosen Publishing, 2005. (MS)

Greatest Stars of the NBA Series[††]

Tokyopop and NBA. *Greatest Stars of the NBA: All-Time Dunks*. NBA Ser. Los Angeles: Tokyopop, 2006. (MS)

Tokyopop and NBA. *Greatest Stars of the NBA: Kevin Garnett*. NBA Ser. Los Angeles: Tokyopop, 2004. (MS)

Tokyopop and NBA. *Greatest Stars of the NBA: Kobe Bryant*. NBA Ser. Los Angeles: Tokyopop, 2007. (MS)

Tokyopop and NBA. *Greatest Starts of the NBA: Shaquille O'Neal*. NBA Ser. Los Angeles: Tokyopop, 2004. (MS)

Tokyopop and NBA. *Greatest Stars of the NBA: Tim Duncan*. NBA Ser. Los Angeles: Tokyopop, 2004. (MS)

Bio-Graphics Series—Magic Wagon[‡‡]

Dunn, Joeming. *Amelia Earhart*. Illustrated by Ben Dunn. Bio-Graphics Ser. Minneapolis, MN: ABDO Publishing, 2009. (MS)

Dunn, Joeming. *Booker T. Washington*. Illustrated by Chris Allen. Bio-Graphics Ser. Minneapolis, MN: ABDO Publishing, 2009. (MS)

Dunn, Joeming. *Clara Barton*. Illustrated by Rod Espinosa. Bio-Graphics Ser. Minneapolis, MN: ABDO Publishing, 2009. (MS)

Dunn, Joeming. *Martin Luther King Jr*. Illustrated by Chris Allen. Bio-Graphics Ser. Minneapolis, MN: ABDO Publishing, 2009. (MS)

Dunn, Joeming. *Sacagawea*. Illustrated by Rod Espinosa. Bio-Graphics Ser. Minneapolis, MN: ABDO Publishing, 2009. (MS)

[**]Additional titles are available in the Graphic Nonfiction Biographies Series.
[††]Additional titles are available in the Greatest Stars of the NBA Series.
[‡‡]Additional titles are available in the Bio-Graphics Series.

Lesson Plans

Lesson Plan Title: Anne Frank

Grade Level: MS

Subject Areas: Social Studies, World History, Biographies

Curriculum Focus/Concepts: Holocaust, World War II, primary and secondary resources

Graphic Novel Tie-In:

The story of Anne Frank is taught in many middle schools, usually in conjunction with reading either Anne Frank's *Diary of a Young Girl*, or the play, *The Diary of Anne Frank* by Frances Goodrich and Albert Hackett. The inclusion of a powerful graphic biography to the lesson will add layers of understanding to any study of Anne Frank and the Holocaust.

Anne Frank: The Anne Frank House Authorized Graphic Biography by Sid Jacobson and Ernie Colon is broader in scope than Anne Frank's actual diary, covering historical and political details before and after the Frank family's years of hiding from the Nazis. This additional information will augment students' understanding of how the Holocaust came to happen and the impact it had on the world. The book gives a balanced view of Anne's personality—her strengths and flaws—and puts her age and personality into perspective, leading to a better understanding of the family's dynamics. One compelling chapter describes what happened to the Franks and their friends after their discovery. The book goes on to explain how Otto Frank published Anne's diary after the war and describes how the Anne Frank House became a museum.

The graphic novel could serve as either an introduction to the topic or be studied afterward, and could be read in part or whole.

Objectives:

Students will understand the causes, events, and impact of the Holocaust.
Students will gain insight into the genocide by the Nazis during World War II.
Students will make connections between historic and modern-day events.

Materials/Resources:
Books
Frank, Anne. *The Diary of a Young Girl*. New York: Bantam, 1993.
Goodrich, Frances and Hackett, Albert. *The Diary of Anne Frank* New York: Dramatists Play Service, 1986.
Jacobsen, Sid and Ernie Colon. *Anne Frank: The Anne Frank House Authorized Graphic Biography*. New York: Hill Y Wang, 2010.

Websites
Anne Frank House website: http://www.annefrank.org/en/

Procedures/Activities:
Have students read one of the versions of Anne Frank's story, along with the graphic novel.
A class discussion, a compare-and-contrast paper, or further research on the Holocaust can follow, if desired.

Discussion Questions:
What motivated Otto Frank's employees to hide the family? What would you have done?
Do you know anyone with a personality similar to Anne's? What were her strengths and weaknesses?
How was the Nazi Party allowed to come into power? Could something like that happen today?
Compare the two versions of Anne's story. What was similar and what was different?
How does the artwork in the graphic novel reflect its topic?
How does the artist's medium and style make the art interdependent with the text?

Closure:
Visit the website of the Anne Frank House.
Have students create a timeline of events during the Holocaust.
Have students watch the videos *They Spoke Out: American Voices Against the Holocaust*, a series of short videos by Disney and ABC News that are told in a combination of photos, video, and comic panels. One video describes Otto Frank's failed efforts to bring his family to America prior to the start of the war. The videos can be found at http://dep.disney.go.com/theyspokeout/index.html.

Extension Activities:
Two other historical fiction graphic novels cover the time period of the Holocaust in a slightly different way. Eric Heuvel's *A Family Secret* (Farrar, Straus, & Giroux, 2009) and *The Search* (Farrar, Straus, & Giroux, 2009), written in conjunction with The Anne Frank House, tell of two friends growing up in the Netherlands during World War II. Though Helena's father supports the Nazis, she attempts to help her Jewish friend, Esther, who manages to run away and hide in the countryside. Esther's parents are not so lucky. The girls' stories are recounted in modern-day times to their grandchildren. The Tintin-like style of art, the "telling a story" narration, and touching endings remove the reader slightly from the horrors of what happened, making the books appropriate for younger readers. A teaching guide is available at Macmillian's website: http://media.us.macmillan.com/teachersguides/9780374464554TG.pdf

Assessment: Assess student projects: papers, timelines, and discussion activities.

Lesson Plan Title: Scientists' Stories

Grade Level: HS

Subject Areas: Science, History, Biographies

Curriculum Focus/Concepts: Various areas of science (physical science, psychology, paleontology)

Graphic Novel Tie-In:

The lives of famous scientists are commonly studied throughout school, with high school students able to take biographical information far beyond simple fact-gathering. When paired with additional research on their lives and their scientific works, graphic biographies of scientists can provide a meaningful, inquiry-filled experience. Graphic novels' illustrations give an added glimpse into the details of historical settings, and those same illustrations can make a complex subject more accessible to students new to the topic.

Jim Ottaviani has written several graphic novels about scientists and their disciplines. Though sometimes limited in scope, his books offer an intimate look at aspects of the individuals' lives that are not always found in more basic biographies. Ottaviani's books encourage critical thinking and problem solving as he, at times, drops the reader into the middle of a story while providing only clues about what happened before or after. This makes readers eager to read more to fill in the blanks and see if their inferences and predictions are correct.

Objectives:

Students will learn about the important contributions of scientists.
Students will explain how scientific theories are developed.
Students will make connections between historic and scientific events.
Students will discuss ideas about scholarship and dedication to research.

Materials/Resources:

Books

Ottaviani, Jim. *Bone Sharps, Cowboys, and Thunder Lizards: A Tale of Edward Drinker Cope, Othniel Charles Marsh, and the Gilded Age of Paleontology: Stories about Scientists.* Ann Arbor, MI: G.T. Labs, 2005.

Ottaviani, Jim. *Dignifying Science: Stories about Women Scientists.* Ann Arbor, MI: G.T. Labs, 2009.

Ottaviani, Jim. *Fallout: J. Robert Oppenheimer, Leo Szilard, and the Political Science of the Atomic Bomb.* Ann Arbor, MI: G.T. Labs, 2001.

Ottaviani, Jim and Leland, Myrick. *Feynman.* New York: First Second Publishing, 2011.

Ottaviani, Jim. *Levitation: Physics and Psychology in the Face of Deception.* Ann Arbor, MI: G.T. Labs, 2007.

Ottaviani, Jim. *Suspended in Language: Niels Bohr's Life, Discoveries, and the Century He Shaped.* Ann Arbor, MI: G.T. Labs, 2009.

Ottaviani, Jim. *Two Fisted Science: Stories about Scientists.* Ann Arbor, MI: G.T. Labs, 2009.

Ottaviani, Jim. *Wire Mothers: Harry Harlow and the Science of Love.* Ann Arbor, MI: G.T. Labs, 2007.

Procedures/Activities:

Have students select a person from the ones featured in the graphic novels. Make students understand that they may know little or nothing about the person, but they will learn as they go.

Give students time to read about the scientist they chose. If students work in pairs, they can discuss what they've read, making inferences and predictions.

Tell students to conduct additional research on the scientists' lives and their works, using print and online resources. Have students locate at least one primary source of information and attempt to find a photo.

Have students create oral presentations or written papers about their findings.

Discussion Questions:

What scientific advances was your person involved with? What were the problems they saw and tried to solve? Why are their accomplishments significant?

Who and what influenced them?

What obstacles did they face, and why? How were the obstacles related to the time period?

How are scientific theories developed? Whose work did your scientist build on? Who went on to build upon his or her work?

If this scientist lived today, how would his or her life would be different? What scientific problems would he or she likely work on?

How does the artwork in the graphic novel reflect its topic?

How does the artist's medium and style make it interdependent with the text?

Closure:

Have students create a timeline of their scientist's life, along with important world events during that time.

Extension Activities:

Visit publisher G.T. Labs' website for more information on Ottaviani's books, including teaching guides. http://www.gt-labs.com/index.html

Assessment: Assess students' reports and timeline, using a rubric.

Chapter 13

Science-Based Graphic Novels in Schools: A Successful Experiment

Introduction

Looking for a colorful and unique way to get your students excited about science? Science-related graphic novels offer a great way to capture the imagination of students, whether they think science is boring or they are destined to be a future astronaut. The combination of text and illustrations in graphic novels can help students understand science information that may be challenging for them when offered through text alone. Along with accurate scientific information, many titles present clearly defined science terms, diagrams, glossaries, and links to websites that can facilitate student learning.

Fortunately, for students and educators, the availability of quality science-based graphic novels is skyrocketing. Librarians and teachers can now access titles on all grade levels that effectively introduce students to scientific concepts, biographies of scientists, and even science careers. From atoms to x-rays, the titles listed below can provide you with an electrifying way to get your students engaged in reading about science. You can also use these and other titles to collaborate with classroom teachers to teach science lessons.

Connecting to the Standards

AASL Standards for the 21st-Century Learner

1.2.3 Demonstrate creativity by using multiple resources and formats.
4.1.4 Seek information for personal learning in a variety of formats and genres.

Comic Connections

- After your middle school students have finished a unit on volcanoes, suggest that they read *Into the Volcano: A Graphic Novel* (Wood, 2008). This fast-paced

The Bottom Line

It is not rocket science—allowing your students to get hands on with science-related graphic novels can help them learn about the science curriculum in exciting new ways.

mystery/adventure is about brothers who go with their cousin to Kokalaha Island, where they meet Aunt Lulu and become trapped in an erupting volcano.

When they finish the book, students can view the pictures of volcanoes on National Geographic's website.

http://environment.nationalgeographic.com/environment/natural-disasters/volcano-profile

They can compare the illustrations in the novel with photography on the website.

- Middle school students will enjoy learning about the scientific adventures of Max Axiom, when they read the Graphic Science series by Capstone. They have never had a science teacher like Max Axiom, a superhero who can travel through time, and shrink to the size of an atom! Difficult topics such as force and motion become less threatening to students, when seen through the x-ray vision eyes of a superhero. There are over 20 titles in the series that can help students learn about science in super new ways.

Suggested Titles for Middle and High Schools (MS & HS)

Abadzis, Nick, and Hilary Sycamore. *Laika.* New York: First Second, 2007. (MS & HS)

Adamson, Thomas K, Gordon Purcell, and Terry Beatty. *The First Moon Landing.* Mankato, MN: Capstone, 2007. (MS)

Brusha, Joe, and Anthony Spay. *Top 10 Deadliest Sharks.* Fort Washington, PA: Silver Dragon, 2010. (MS) *To be followed by Discovery Channel's graphic novels, *Dinosaurs & Prehistoric Predators*, and *Animal Planet's World* in 2011.

Charles Darwin's On the Origin of Species: A Graphic Adaptation. Adapted by Michael Keller and illustrated by Nicholle Rager, 2009. (HS)

Davis, Eleanor. *The Secret Science Alliance and the Copycat Crook.* New York: Bloomsbury, 2009. (MS)

Himuro, Isao, and Kotaro Iwasaki. *Einstein.* Edu-Manga. Carson, CA: Digital Manga, 2006. (MS)

Hosler, Jay. *Clan Apis.* Columbus, OH: Active Synapse, 2000. (HS)

Hosler, Jay, Kevin Cannon, and Zander Cannon. *Evolution: The Story of Life on Earth.* New York: Hill and Wang, 2011. (HS)

Jeffrey, Gary, and Mike Lacey. *Incredible Space Missions.* New York: Rosen Central, 2008. (MS)

Ottaviani, Jim. *Bone Sharps, Cowboys, and Thunder Lizards: A Tale of Edwin Drinker Cope, Othniel Charles Marsh, and the Gilded Age of Paleontology.* Ann Arbor, MI: G.T. Labs, 2005. (HS)

Ottaviani, Jim, and Donna Barr. *Dignifying Science: Stories About Women Scientists.* Ann Arbor, MI: G.T. Labs, 2003. (HS)

Ottaviani, Jim. *Fallout: J. Robert Oppenheimer, Leo Szilard, and the Political Science of the Atomic Bomb*. Ann Arbor, MI: G.T. Labs, 2001. (HS)

Ottaviani, Jim, Zander Cannon, and Kevin Cannon. *T-minus: The Race to the Moon*. New York: Aladdin, 2009. (MS & HS)

Ottaviani, Jim, and Mark Badger. *Two-fisted Science: Stories about Scientists*. Ann Arbor, MI: G.T. Labs, 2001. (HS)

Schultz, Mark, Zander Cannon, and Kevin Cannon. *The Stuff of Life: A Graphic Guide to Genetics and DNA*. New York: Hill and Wang, 2009. (HS)

Wood, Don. *Into the Volcano: A Graphic Novel*. New York: The Blue Sky Press, 2008. (MS & HS)

Suggested Titles in a Series

The Cartoon Guide Series

Gonick, Larry, and Alice B. Outwater. *The Cartoon Guide to the Environment*. Cartoon Guide Ser. New York: HarperCollins Publishers, 1996. (HS)

Gonick, Larry, and Art Huffman. *The Cartoon Guide to Physics*. Cartoon Guide Ser. New York: HarperPerennial, 1991. (HS)

Gonick, Larry, and Craig Criddle. *The Cartoon Guide to Chemistry*. Cartoon Guide Ser. New York: HarperResource, 2005. (HS)

Gonick, Larry, and Mark Wheelis. *The Cartoon Guide to Genetics*. Cartoon Guide Ser. New York: Harper Perennial, 1991. (HS)

*Dinosaurs Series**

Bachin, Matteo. *Giant Vs. Giant: Argentinosaurus*. Dinosaur Ser. New York: Abbeville Kids, 2010. (MS & HS)

Bacchin, Matteo. *The Hunting Pack: Allosaurus*. Dinosaur Ser. Abbeville Press: New York; London, 2010. (MS & HS)

Bacchin, Matteo, and Marco Signore. *A Jurassic Mystery: Archaeopteryx*. Dinosaur Ser. New York: Abbeville Press, 2008. (MS & HS)

Bacchin, Matteo, and Marco Signore. *The Journey: Plateosaurus*. Dinosaur Ser. New York: Abbeville Press, 2008. (MS & HS)

Bacchin, Matteo, and Marco Signore. *T. Rex and the Great Extinction*. Dinosaur Ser. New York: Abbeville Kids, 2010. (MS & HS)

Environmental Dangers Series†

Faust, Daniel R. *Energy Crisis: The Future of Fossil Fuels*. Environmental Dangers Ser. New York: PowerKids Press, 2009. (MS)

Faust, Daniel R. *Global Warming: Greenhouse Gases and the Ozone Layer*. Environmental Dangers Ser. New York: PowerKids Press, 2009. (MS)

Faust, Daniel R. *Sinister Sludge: Oil Spills and the Environment*. Environmental Dangers Ser. New York: PowerKids Press, 2009. (MS)

Nelson, John. *Collision Course: Asteroids and Earth*. Environmental Dangers Ser. New York: PowerKids Press, 2008. (MS)

---

*Additional titles are available in the Dinosaurs Series.
†Additional titles are available in the Environmental Dangers Series.

Nelson, John. *Polar Ice Caps in Danger: Expedition to Antarctica.* Environmental Dangers Ser. New York: PowerKids Press, 2009. (MS)

Graphic Adventures: The Human Body[‡]

Dunn, Joeming W., and Rod Espinosa. *The Brain: A Graphic Novel Tour.* Graphic Adventures Ser. Edina, MN: Magic Wagon, 2010. (MS)

Dunn, Joeming W., and Rod Espinosa. *The Eyes: A Graphic Novel Tour.* Graphic Adventures Ser. Edina, MN: Magic Wagon, 2010. (MS)

Dunn, Joeming W., and Rod Espinosa. *The Heart: A Graphic Novel Tour.* Graphic Adventures Ser. Edina, MN: Magic Wagon, 2010. (MS)

Dunn, Joeming W., and Rod Espinosa. *The Kidneys: A Graphic Novel Tour.* Graphic Adventures Ser. Edina, MN: Magic Wagon, 2010. (MS)

Dunn, Joeming W., and Rod Espinosa. *The Lungs: A Graphic Novel Tour.* Graphic Adventures Ser. Edina, MN: Magic Wagon, 2010. (MS)

Graphic Dinosaurs Series[§]

Shone, Rob. *Diplodocus: The Whip-Tailed Dinosaur.* Graphic Dinosaurs Ser. New York: PowerKids, 2009. (MS)

Shone, Rob. *Triceratops: The Three Horned Dinosaur.* Graphic Dinosaurs Ser. New York: PowerKids Press, 2008. (MS)

Shone, Rob. *Tyrannosaurus: The Tyrant Lizard.* Graphic Dinosaurs Ser. New York: PowerKids Press, 2008. (MS)

West, David. *Pteranodon: Giant of the Sky.* Graphic Dinosaurs Ser. New York: PowerKids Press, 2008. (MS)

West, David, and James Field. *Velociraptor: The Speedy Thief.* Graphic Dinosaurs Ser. New York: PowerKids Press, 2008. (MS)

Graphic Discoveries Series[**]

Jeffrey, Gary. *The History of Flight.* Graphic Discoveries Ser. New York: Rosen Central, 2008. (MS)

Jeffrey, Gary. *Medical Breakthroughs.* Graphic Discoveries Ser. New York: Rosen Central, 2008. (MS)

Jeffrey, Gary, and Mike Lacey. *Incredible Space Missions.* Graphic Discoveries Ser. New York: Rosen Central, 2008. (MS)

Shone, Rob. *Fantastic Fossils.* Graphic Discoveries Ser. New York: Rosen Central, 2008. (MS)

Shone, Rob, and Nick Spender. *Ancient Treasures.* Graphic Discoveries Ser. New York: Rosen Pub. Group, 2008. (MS)

Graphic Forensic Science[††]

Jeffrey, Gary, and Terry Riley. *Autopsies: Pathologists at Work.* Graphic Forensic Science Ser. New York: Rosen Central, 2008. (MS)

[‡]Additional titles are available in the Graphic Adventures: The Human Body Series.
[§]Additional titles are available in the Graphic Dinosaurs Series.
[**]Additional titles are available in the Graphic Discoveries Series.
[††]Additional titles are available in the Graphic Forensic Science Series.

Jeffrey, Gary, and Peter Richardson. *Solving Crimes with Trace Evidence*. Graphic Forensic Science Ser. New York: Rosen Central, 2008. (MS)

Shone, Rob, and Nik Spender. *Corpses and Skeletons: The Science of Forensic Anthropology*. Graphic Forensic Science Ser. New York: Rosen Pub. Group, 2008. (MS)

Shone, Rob. *Crime Scene Investigators*. Graphic Forensic Science Ser. New York: Rosen Pub. Group, 2008. (MS)

West, David. *Detective Work with Ballistics*. Graphic Forensic Science Ser. New York: Rosen Pub. Group, 2008. (MS)

Graphic Natural Disasters[‡‡]

Jeffrey, Gary, and Mike Lacey. *Hurricanes*. Graphic Natural Disasters Ser. New York: Rosen Pub. Group, 2007. (MS)

Jeffrey, Gary, and Terry Riley. *Tornadoes & Superstorms*. Graphic Natural Disasters Ser. New York: Rosen Pub. Group, 2007. (MS)

Shone, Rob. *Avalanches & Landslides*. Graphic Natural Disasters Ser. New York: Rosen Pub. Group, 2007. (MS)

Shone, Rob. *Volcanoes*. Graphic Natural Disasters Ser. New York: Rosen Pub. Group, 2007. (MS)

Shone, Rob, and Nik Spender. *Earthquakes*. Graphic Natural Disasters Ser. New York: Rosen Pub. Group, 2007. (MS)

Graphic Science Series[§§]

Biskup, Agnieszka, and Tod Smith. *Exploring Ecosystems with Max Axiom, Super Scientist*. Graphic Library Ser. Mankato, MN: Capstone Press, 2007. (MS)

Krohn, Katherine E., Tod Smith, and A. Milgrom. *The Earth-Shaking Facts About Earthquakes with Max Axiom, Super Scientist*. Graphic Library Ser. Mankato, MN: Capstone Press, 2008. (MS)

Sohn, Emily, Steve Erwin, and Charles Barnett. *A Crash Course in Forces and Motion with Max Axiom, Super Scientist*. Graphic Library Ser. Mankato, MN: Capstone Press, 2007. (MS)

Sohn, Emily, and Nick Derington. *The Illuminating World of Light with Max Axiom, Super Scientist*. Graphic Library Ser. Mankato, MN: Capstone Press, 2008. (MS)

Inventions and Discovery Series[***]

Anderson, Jameson, and Steve Erwin. *The Z-Boys and Skateboarding*. Inventions and Discovery Ser. Mankato, MN: Capstone Press, 2008. (MS)

Fandel, Jennifer, and Keith Tucker. *Alexander Graham Bell and the Telephone*. Inventions and Discovery Ser. Mankato, MN: Capstone Press, 2007. (MS)

Krohn, Katherine E., and A. Milgrom. *Jonas Salk and the Polio Vaccine*. Inventions and Discovery Ser. Mankato, MN: Capstone Press, 2007. (MS)

O'Hearn, Michael. *Henry Ford and the Model T*. Inventions and Discovery Ser. Mankato, MN: Capstone Press, 2007. (MS)

O'Hearn, Michael, Ron Frenz, and Charles Barnett. *Jake Burton Carpenter and the Snowboard*. Inventions and Discovery Ser. Mankato, MN: Capstone Press, 2007. (MS)

[‡‡]Additional titles are available in the Graphic Natural Disasters Series.
[§§]Additional titles are available in the Graphic Science Series.
[***]Additional titles are available in the Inventions and Discovery Series.

Manga Guide To . . . Series

Fujitaki, Kazuhiro. *The Manga Guide to Electricity.* Manga Guide Ser. San Francisco: No Starch Press, 2009. (HS)

Nitta, Hideo, and Keita Takatsu. *The Manga Guide to Physics.* Manga Guide Ser. San Francisco, CA: No Starch Press, 2009. (HS)

Takemura, Masaharu. *The Manga Guide to Molecular Biology.* Manga Guide Ser. San Francisco, CA: No Starch Press, 2009. (HS)

Superheroes on a Medical Mission[†††]

Chilman-Blair, Kim, and John Taddeo. *Medikidz Explain Asthma.* New York: Rosen Publishing's Rosen Central, 2010. (MS)

Chilman-Blair, Kim, and John Taddeo. *Medikidz Explain Diabetes.* New York: Rosen Publishing's Rosen Central, 2010. (MS)

Chilman-Blair, Kim, and John Taddeo. *Medikidz Explain Epilepsy.* New York: Rosen Publishing's Rosen Central, 2010. (MS)

Chilman-Blair, Kim, and John Taddeo. *Medikidz Explain Scoliosis.* New York: Rosen Publishing's Rosen Central, 2010. (MS)

Lesson Plans

Lesson Plan Title: Space Exploration

Grade Level: MS

Subject Area: Science

Curriculum Focus/Concepts: Earth and Space Science, Space exploration, History of space exploration

Graphic Novel Tie-Ins:

The four graphic novels used with this lesson cover the topic of space exploration, each from a unique perspective.

The First Moon Landing by Elizabeth Hudson-Goff and Dale Anderson describes Neil Armstrong's Apollo 11 landing on the moon. The book, through large, cleanly drawn illustrations and simple text, gives background information, describes the landing, and explains what followed after. It includes a further reading section and a list of related websites.

Incredible Space Missions by Gary Jeffrey focuses on the space race as the United States and the Soviet Union developed the technology to walk in space and land on the moon. The book is broken into short chapters on different topics, and goes into more depth than the previous book. Included are photos, realistic drawings of space technology, a glossary, a "for more information" page, and an index.

Longer and more complex, *Laika,* by Nick Abadzis, is a fictionalized account of the first dog in space. It is a fascinating, poignant story of the Russian space program, the

---

[†††]Additional titles are available in the Superheroes on a Medical Mission Series.

people who played a role in the launch of Sputnik II, and Laika, the dog that was sent into space without a way back. The book contains an afterword and a bibliography.

T-Minus: the Race To the Moon by Jim Ottaviani, Zander Cannon, and Kevin Cannon, is written on a more-advanced level, but still accessible to younger adolescents. This fictionalized account of the space race is packed with information and detail. The black and white illustrations give the book a sense of the time period, and additional resources are listed in the back of the book.

Objectives:
Students will trace major events in the U.S. space exploration program from the 1960s to the present.
Students will compare and contrast the space programs in the United States and the Soviet Union.
Students will discuss how space exploration has affected life on earth.
Students will discuss the issues surrounding the use of animals in space science.

Materials/Resources:
Books
Stone, Tanya Lee. *Almost Astronauts: 13 Women Who Dared to Dream*. Somerville, MA: Candlewick. 2009.
Dyson, Marianne J. *Space Station Science: Life in Free Fall*. Minneapolis, MN: Windward Publishing. 2004.

Websites
National Air and Space Administration's website on Space Exploration http://solarsystem.nasa.gov/educ/howweexplore.cfm
National Air and Space Administration's website on Space Flight http://spaceflight.nasa.gov/home/index.html
Space Today Online's website on the history of animals in space http://www.spacetoday.org/Astronauts/Animals/Dogs.html

Procedure/Activities:
Present the students with an overview of the history of space exploration from the 1960s to the present.
Show them NASA's website that provides the history of their launch and station programs.
Break the students into literature circles.
Name each group after one of the space shuttles (Columbia, Challenger, Discovery, Atlantis, Endeavor) and/or other space-related terms.
Have each group read one or more of the graphic novel tie-in titles.
Have each group create a poster of five fun facts about space exploration that they learned from the graphic novels and websites.

Discussion Questions:
In 1962, President John F. Kennedy said in a speech, "In a very real sense, it will not be one man going to the moon it will be an entire nation. For all of us must work to put him there." What did President Kennedy mean by that quote?

What impact has space exploration had on your lives?

Some people think that too much funding is spent on funding the space program. Do you agree or disagree?

Do you think animals should be used in space exploration programs? Why/why not?

How does the artwork in the graphic novels reflect their topics?

How does each artist's medium and style make the art interdependent with the text?

Closure:

Have students discuss the impact of space exploration on their lives, and what they think the future of the space exploration program will be in the United States.

Extension Activities:

Break the students into their literature circle groups to learn about space-related careers and the International Space Station.

Have each group select one space career from the list found at the bottom of this handout from the Learn NC website: www.learnnc.org/lp/media/uploads/2008/01/iss_student.pdf.

Using the following resources, have the students answer the questions on the handout regarding space careers and the International Space Station,

- Rosen career books
- Other career books available in your library collection
- The following websites:
  - Occupational Outlook Handbook website (http://www.bls.gov/oco)
  - NASA Astroventure website (http://astroventure.arc.nasa.gov)
  - Websites about the International Space Station that are listed on the handout

Assessment:

Assess each group's poster, as well as participation in the groups.

Lesson Plan Title: The Human Genome Project

Grade Level: HS

Subject Area: Science

Curriculum Focus/Concepts: Biology, Genetics, DNA, Human Genome Project

Graphic Novel Tie-Ins:

DNA, genetics, and the Human Genome project are challenging subjects for high school students. The treatment of these topics in textbooks is often difficult for students to follow. There are currently two graphic novel titles that can supplement the material found in science textbooks. Viewing the illustrations in these books makes the content less intimidating, and can help some students have a scientific "aha" moment.

In the book, *The Manga Guide to Molecular Biology* (Sakura, 2009), Dr. Moro provides Rin and Ami with a special virtual machine to travel inside the human body. There, they get a first-hand look at the world of molecular biology. When students read this book, they will learn about the complex world of molecular biography broken down into small pieces. Practical examples, combined with the manga style, can provide students with an understanding of a topic that may have previously seemed alien to them.

Similarly, *The Stuff of Life: A Graphic Guide to Genetics and DNA* (Schultz, Cannon, & Cannon, 2009), is an informative and easy to read look at molecular biology and the world of genetics. This, often humorous, book is about Bloort 183, an asexual scientist on a dying planet charged with researching the fundamentals of human DNA and evolution and boiling it all down into clear, simple language. Whether you are teaching basic biology or an Advanced Placement class, this book will make the topic of human genetics less confusing for you and your students.

Objectives:
Students will develop an understanding of the Human Genome Project, its history and development Students will describe how the Human Genome Project contributes to an understanding of our species, as well as other species.
Students will learn how the Human Genome Project contributes to the field of medicine.

Materials/Resources:
Books
Watson, James. D., & Berry Andrew. *DNA: The Secret of Life*. New York: Knopf, 2004.

Handout
Human Genome Project www.nih.gov/about/researchresultsforthepublic/HumanGenomeProject.pdf

Websites
The Human Genome Project http://www.genome.gov/10001772
Human Genome Project Information http://www.ornl.gov/sci/techresources/Human
    _Genome/home.shtml
NOVA Video of the Human Genome Project http://www.teachersdomain.org/asset/
    tdc02_vid_hgp_dvs

Procedure/Activities:
This lesson should follow a unit on DNA and Genetics so that students will have an understanding of DNA and genomes before the lesson begins.
Provide the students with a brief overview of the Human Genome Project by showing them pages 98–101 in *The Stuff of Life* (Schulz, 2009).
Break the students into groups and tell them that each group will be preparing a poster on the Human Genome Project to present in class.
Show the students the NOVA video of the Human Genome Project (listed above).
Provide the groups with time to review the handout, the graphic novels, other nonfiction books, and websites that contain information about the Human Genome Project.

Provide each group with poster paper, markers, and so on to prepare the poster that they will present to their classmates. Allow the groups enough time to complete the posters, followed by time for the poster presentations.

Discussion Questions:
What is a genome and why is it important?
How has the Human Genome Project improved our understanding of human genetics?
Do you think that most people are in favor of the Human Genome Project? If so, explain why. If not, explain why people would oppose the project.
How does the artwork in the graphic novels reflect their topics?
How does each artist's medium and style make the art interdependent with the text?

Closure:
Have students describe the ways in which the Human Genome Project affects medicine today, and how they think it will affect medicine in the future.

Extension Activities:
Provide the students with class time to visit the following websites regarding ethical, legal, and social issues related to the Human Genome Project:
http://www.ornl.gov/sci/techresources/Human_Genome/elsi/elsi.shtml
http://www.ornl.gov/sci/techresources/Human_Genome/publicat/tko/08_ethical.html
http://www.actionbioscience.org/genomic/carroll_ciaffa.html
After examining the websites, have students write a 1–2 page paper describing two of these issues. Allow time for a class discussion about the issues the students researched on the websites.

Assessment:
Assess each group's poster, as well as their participation in the groups.

Chapter 14

Don't Know Much about History: Teaching Social Studies with Graphic Novels

Introduction

The explosive increase of nonfiction books published in the graphic format makes it easy to locate historically accurate, acclaimed graphic novels that teach and enrich many of the topics studied in middle and high school social studies. You have a continuum of choices as to exactly how to use a graphic novel to support social studies instruction—everything from displaying a small portion of it as an introduction to a topic, to reading the graphic novel in its entirety. Because of the engaging format, graphic novels complement the use of sometimes-dry textbooks. Students less proficient at reading nonfiction won't be as threatened by graphic novels because the context clues supplied by the images give readers concrete, tangible information about the time period, events, and people. In fact, nonfiction historic graphic novels immerse readers of all levels of proficiency in the events of the past. They show vivid details about the architecture, dress, standard of living, technology, and physical characteristics of famous people in the same way a movie does, making the time period come alive and giving students a real feel for what life was like during those times. Students can feel a sense of engagement in events of the past and better imagine exactly what it was like to live during the Siege of Troy, the Civil War, or the Montgomery Bus Boycott.

This chapter contains lesson plans that can be adapted for other grade levels, because some historic topics are covered in both middle and high school. In addition, teaching guides and lesson plans can be found for acclaimed books like *Maus: A Survivor's Tale* by Art Spiegleman and Marjane Satrapi's *Persepolis*, at publishers' sites and lesson plan websites. The Comic Connections section contains links to some of these, plus ideas for pairing graphic novels with topics you may already teach.

Connecting to the Standards

AASL Standards for the 21st-Century Learner

2.1.3 Use strategies to draw conclusions from information and apply knowledge to curricular areas, real-world situations, and further investigations.

National Standards for History

Historical Thinking Standard 3 The student engages in historical analysis and interpretation.

Comic Connections

- Pair Brian K. Vaughan and Niko Henrichon's graphic novel *Pride of Baghdad*, which describes the destruction of the Baghdad Zoo during the Iraq War, with Mark Alan Stamaty's *Alia's Mission: Saving the Books of Iraq*, a story of one librarian's daring rescue of Iraq's books.
- Use the teaching guide for *The Storm in the Barn* by Matt Phelan, found at http://www.candlewick.com/book_files/0763636185.btg.1.pdf, along with the Library of Congress's lesson plan on The Dust Bowl, at http://memory.loc.gov/learn/lessons/99/dust/intro.html.
- Enrich a unit on the exploration of America with *Lewis & Clark* by Nick Bertozzi and *Journey Into Mohawk Country* by George O'Connor, a retelling, in his own words, of little-known explorer Harmen Meyndertsz van den Bogaert's travels into upstate New York.
- Teach about Rosa Parks and the Montgomery Bus Boycott, using the many graphic novels available, including *Rosa Parks and the Montgomery Bus Boycott* by Connie Colwell Miller, *The Montgomery Bus Boycott* by Kerri O'Hern, and *Rosa Parks: the Life of a Civil Rights Heroine* by Rob Shone and Nick Spender. Supplement with primary sources from the Teaching Tolerance site at http://www.tolerance.org/activity/bus-boycott-historical-documents-highlig.
- Use the teaching guide for *Maus: A Survivor's Tale: My Father Bleeds History*, located on Random House's website at http://www.randomhouse.com/highschool/catalog/display.pperl?isbn=9780394747231&view=tg.
- Make use of Hill and Wang's Teacher's Guide for *The 9/11 Report: a Graphic Adaptation* to better analyze the events of September 11. The guide can be found at http://media.us.macmillan.com/teachersguides/9780809057399TG.pdf.

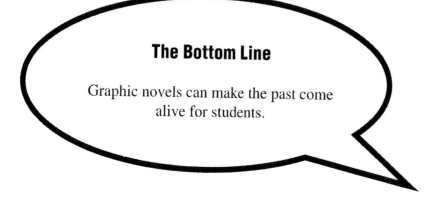

The Bottom Line

Graphic novels can make the past come alive for students.

Suggested Titles by Middle and High School

Abadzis, Nick. *Laika*. New York: First Second, 2007. (MS & HS)

Bertozzi, Nick. *Lewis & Clark*. New York: First Second, 2011. (HS)

Butzer, C. M. *Gettysburg: the Graphic Novel*. New York: Bowen Press/Collins, 2009. (MS)

Geary, Rick. *The Lindbergh Child*. New York: NBM Comics Lit, 2008. (HS)

Geary, Rick. *Trotsky: A Graphic Biography*. New York: Hill and Wang, 2009. (HS)

Guibert, Emmanuel. *Alan's War: the Memories of G.I. Alan Cope*. New York: First Second, 2008. (HS)

Helfer, Andrew. *Malcolm X: A Graphic Biography*. New York: Hill and Wang, 2006. (HS)

Hennessey, Jonathan, and Aaron McConnell. *The United States Constitution: A Graphic Adaptation*. New York: Hill and Wang, 2008. (MS &HS)

Heuvel, Eric. *A Family Secret*. New York: Farrar Straus Giroux, 2009. (MS)

Heuvel, Eric. *The Search*. New York: Farrar Straus Giroux, 2009. (MS)

Jacobson, Sidney, and Ernie Colón. *Anne Frank: the Anne Frank House Authorized Graphic Biography*. New York: Hill and Wang, 2006. (MS & HS)

Jacobson, Sidney. *After 9/11: America's War on Terror (2001)*. New York: Hill and Wang, 2008. (HS)

Jacobson, Sidney, and Ernie Colón. *The 9/11 Report: A Graphic Adaptation*. New York: Hill and Wang, 2006. (MS & HS)

Kim, Susan, and Laurence Klavan. *City of Spies*. New York: First Second, 2010. (MS)

Kouno, Fumiyo. *Town of Evening Calm: Country of Cherry Blossoms*. San Francisco, CA: Last Gasp, 2007. (HS)

Kubert, Joe. *Yossel*. New York: Vertigo Comics, 2011. (HS)

Lagos, Alexander, and Joseph Lagos. *The Sons of Liberty*. New York: Random House Children's Books, 2010. (MS & HS)

Lat. *Kampung Boy*. New York: First Second, 2006. (MS)

Lat. *Town Boy*. New York: First Second, 2007. (MS)

Love, Jeremy. *Bayou. Volume One*. New York: DC Comics, 2009. (HS)

Lutes, Jason, and Nick Bertozzi. *Houdini: the Handcuff King*. New York: Hyperion, 2007. (MS)

Mack, Stan, and Susan Champlin. *Road to Revolution!* New York: Bloomsbury, 2009. (MS)

Miller, Frank, and Lynn Varley. *300*. Milwaukie, OR: Dark Horse Comics, 1999. (HS)

Neufeld, Josh. *A. D.: New Orleans After the Deluge*. New York: Pantheon Books, 2009. (HS)

O'Connor, George, and, Harmen Meyndertsz Van den Bogaert. *Journey Into Mohawk Country*. New York: First Second, 2006. (HS)

Ottaviani, Jim. *Fallout: J. Robert Oppenheimer, Leo Szilard, and the Political Science of the Atomic Bomb*. Ann Arbor, MI: G.T. Labs, 2001. (HS)

Ottaviani, Jim. *T-Minus: the Race to the Moon*. New York: Aladdin, 2009. (MS & HS)

Phelan, Matt. *The Storm in the Barn*. Somerville, MA: Candlewick Press, 2009. (MS)

Poe, Marshall. *A House Divided*. New York: Aladdin Paperbacks, 2009. (MS)

Poe, Marshall. *Sons of Liberty*. New York: Aladdin Paperbacks, 2008. (MS)

Poe, Marshall, and Ellen Lindner. *Little Rock Nine*. New York: Aladdin Paperbacks, 2008. (MS & HS)

Sacco, Joe. *Palestine*. Seattle WA: Fantagraphics Books, 2007. (HS)

Satrapi, Marjane. *Persepolis*. New York: Pantheon Books, 2003. (MS & HS)

Satrapi, Marjane. *Persepolis 2: The Story of a Return*. New York: Pantheon Books, 2003. (MS & HS)

Shanower, Eric. *Age of Bronze*. Orange, CA: Image, 2001. (MS &HS)

Speigelman, Art. *Maus: A Survivor's Tale*. New York: Pantheon Books, 1986. (MS and HS)

Speigelman, Art. *Maus II: A Survivor's Tale: and Here My Troubles Began*. New York: Pantheon Books, 1991. (MS and HS)

Sturm, James, and Rich Tommaso. *Satchel Paige: Striking Out Jim Crow*. New York: Hyperion, 2007. (MS & HS)

Vaughan, Brian and Niko Henrichon. *Pride of Baghdad*. New York: DC Comics, 2006. (HS)

Zimmerman, Dwight Jon. *The Vietnam War: a Graphic History*. New York: Hill and Wang, 2009. (HS)

Suggested Titles in a Series

The Cartoon History Series

Gonick, Larry. *The Cartoon History of the Universe: Volumes 1–7 From the Big Bang to Alexander the Great*. Cartoon History Ser. New York: W. W. Norton, 1990. (MS & HS)

Gonick, Larry. *The Cartoon History of the Universe II: Volumes 8–13 From the Springtime of China to Fall of Rome*. Cartoon History Ser. New York: Doubleday, 1994. (MS & HS)

Gonick, Larry. *The Cartoon History of the Universe III: From the Rise of Arabia to the Renaissance*. Cartoon History Ser. New York: W. W. Norton, 2002. (MS & HS)

Gonick, Larry. *The Cartoon History of the Modern World Part I: From Columbus to the U.S. Constitution*. Cartoon History Ser. New York: HarperCollins, 2007. (MS & HS)

Gonick, Larry. *The Cartoon History of the Modern World Part II: From the Bastille to the Baghdad*. Cartoon History Ser. New York: HarperCollins, 2009. (MS & HS)

Gonick, Larry. *The Cartoon History of the United States*. Cartoon History Ser. New York: HarperPerennial, 1991. (MS & HS)

Graphic Battles of the Civil War Series

Abnett, Dan. *The Battle of Gettysburg: Blood Spilled on Sacred Ground*. Illustrated by Dheeraj Verma. Graphic Battles of the Civil War Ser. New York: Rosen Publishing, 2007. (MS)

Abnett, Dan. *The Battle of the Wilderness: Deadly Inferno*. Illustrated by Dheeraj Verma. Graphic Battles of the Civil War Ser. New York: Rosen Publishing, 2007. (MS)

Abnett, Dan. *The Monitor versus the Merrimac: Ironclads at Sea*. Illustrated by Dheeraj Verma. Graphic Battles of the Civil War Ser. New York: Rosen Publishing, 2007. (MS)

Hama, Larry. *The Battle of Antietam: "The Bloodiest Day of Battle."* Illustrated by Scott Moore. Graphic Battles of the Civil War Ser. New York: Rosen Publishing, 2007. (MS)

Hama, Larry. *The Battle of First Bull Run: The Civil War Begins*. Illustrated by Scott Moore. Graphic Battles of the Civil War Ser. New York: Rosen Publishing, 2007. (MS)

Hama, Larry. *The Battle of Shiloh: Surprise Attack!* Illustrated by Scott Moore. Graphic Battles of the Civil War Ser. New York: Rosen Publishing, 2007. (MS)

Graphic Battles of the World War II Series

Cain, Bill. *The Battle of the Bulge: Turning Back Hitler's Final Push*. Illustrated by Dheeraj Verma. Graphic Battles of the World War II Ser. New York: Rosen Publishing Group, 2008. (MS)

Hama, Larry. *The Battle of Guadalcanal: Land and Sea Warfare in the South Pacific*. Illustrated by Anthony Williams. Graphic Battles of the World War II Ser. New York: Rosen Publishing Group, 2007. (MS)

Hama, Larry. *The Battle of Iwo Jima: Guerilla Warfare in the Pacific*. Illustrated by Anthony Williams. Graphic Battles of the World War II Ser. New York: Rosen Publishing Group, 2007. (MS)

Murray, Doug. *D-Day: The Liberation of Europe Begins*. Illustrated by Anthony Williams. Graphic Battles of the World War II Ser. New York: Rosen Publishing Group, 2008. (MS)

White, Steve. *The Battle of Midway: The Destruction of the Japanese Fleet*. Illustrated by Richard Elson. Graphic Battles of the World War II Ser. New York: Rosen Publishing Group, 2007. (MS)

White, Steve. *Pearl Harbor: A Day of Infamy*. Illustrated by Jerrold Spahm. Graphic Battles of the World War II Ser. New York: Rosen Publishing Group, 2007. (MS)

Graphic Biography Series*

Braun, Eric. *Booker T. Washington: Great American Educator*. Illustrated by Cynthia Martin. Graphic Biographies Ser. Mankato, MN: Capstone Press, 2006. (MS)

Glaser, Jason. *Jackie Robinson: Baseball's Great Pioneer*. Illustrated by Bob Lentz. Graphic Biographies Ser. Mankato, MN: Capstone Press, 2006. (MS)

Jacobson, Ryan. *Eleanor Roosevelt: First Lady of the World*. Illustrated by Eleanor Schulz. Graphic Biographies Ser. Mankato, MN: Capstone Press, 2006. (MS)

Robbins, Trina. *Bessie Coleman: Daring Stunt Pilot*. Illustrated by Ken Steacy. Graphic Biographies Ser. Mankato, MN: Capstone Press, 2007. (MS)

Robbins, Trina. *Elizabeth Blackwell: America's First Woman Doctor*. Illustrated by Cynthia Martin. Graphic Biographies Ser. Mankato, MN: Capstone Press, 2007. (MS)

Graphic Biographies Series†

Hudson-Goff, Elizabeth, and Jonatha Brown. *Anne Frank*. Illustrated by Guus Floor, D. McHargue, and Jonathan Timmons. Graphic Biographies Ser. New York: Gareth Publishing, 2005. (MS)

O'Hern, Kerri, and Gini Holland. *Louis Armstrong*. Illustrated by Alex Campbell. Graphic Biographies Ser. New York: Gareth Publishing, 2005. (MS)

O'Hern, Kerri, and Gini Holland. *Nelson Mandela*. Illustrated by D. McHargue. Graphic Biographies Ser. New York: Gareth Publishing, 2005. (MS)

O'Hern, Kerri, and Gretchen Will Mayo. *The Wright Brothers*. Illustrated by Rebekah Isaacs and Jonathan Timmons. Graphic Biographies Ser. New York: Gareth Publishing, 2005. (MS)

O'Hern, Kerri, and Lucia Raatma. *Jackie Robinson*. Illustrated by Alex Campbell and Anthony Spay. Graphic Biographies Ser. New York: Gareth Publishing, 2005. (MS)

Graphic Discoveries Series‡

Jeffrey, Gary. *The History of Flight*. Graphic Discoveries Ser. New York: Rosen Central, 2008. (MS)

Shone, Rob, and Nick Spender. *Ancient Treasures*. Graphic Discoveries Ser. New York: Rosen Pub. Group, 2008. (MS)

Graphic Histories Series

Hudson-Goff, Elizabeth, Michael V. Uscha, and Guus Floor. *The Bombing of Pearl Harbor*. Graphic Histories Ser. Milwaukee, WI: World Almanac Library, 2006. (MS)

Hudson-Goff, Elizabeth, Michael V. Uscha, and Guus Floor. *The California Gold Rush*. Graphic Histories Ser. Milwaukee, WI: World Almanac Library, 2006. (MS)

---

*Additional titles are available in the Graphic Biography Series.

†Additional titles are available in the Graphic Biographies Series.

‡Additional titles are available in the Graphic Discoveries Series.

O'Hern, Kerri, and Dale Anderson. *The Battle of Gettysburg*. Graphic Histories Ser. Milwaukee, WI: World Almanac Library, 2006. (MS)

O'Hern, Kerri, and Dale Anderson. *The First Moon Landing*. Graphic Histories Ser. Milwaukee, WI: World Almanac Library, 2006. (MS)

O'Hern Kerri, Frank Walsh, and D. McHargue. *The Montgomery Bus Boycott*. Graphic Histories Ser. Milwaukee, WI: World Almanac Library, 2006. (MS)

O'Hern, Kerri, Janet Riehecky, and D. McHargue. *The Battle of the Alamo*. Graphic Histories Ser. Milwaukee, WI: World Almanac Library, 2006. (MS)

Graphic History Series[§]

Burgan, Michael, Gordon Purcell, and Terry Beatty. *The Creation of the U.S. Constitution*. Graphic History Ser. Mankato, MN: Capstone Press, 2007. (MS)

Burgan, Michael, Richard Dominguez, Bob Wiacek, and Charles Barnett III. *Nat Turner's Slave Rebellion*. Graphic History Ser. Mankato, MN: Capstone Press, 2006. (MS)

Burgan, Michael, Steve Erwin, Keith Williams, and Charles Barnett, III. *The Battle of Gettysburg*. Graphic History Ser. Mankato, MN: Capstone Press, 2006. (MS)

Martin, Michael. *Harriet Tubman and the Underground Railroad*. Graphic History Ser. Mankato, MN: Capstone Press, 2005. (MS)

Miller, Connie Colwell. *Rosa Parks and the Montgomery Bus Boycott*. Graphic History Ser. Mankato, MN: Capstone Press, 2007. (MS)

Olson, Kay Melchisedech, Otha Zackariah, and Edward Lohse. *The Assassination of Abraham Lincoln*. Graphic History Ser. Mankato, MN: Capstone Press, 2005. (MS)

Graphic Nonfiction Biographies Series[**]

Jeffrey, Gary. *Martin Luther King: The Life of a Civil Rights Leader*. Illustrated by Chris Forsey. Graphic Nonfiction Biographies Ser. New York: Rosen Publishing Group, 2007. (MS)

Shone, Rob. *Muhammad Ali: The Life of a Boxing Hero*. Illustrated by Nick Spender. Graphic Nonfiction Biographies Ser. New York: Rosen Publishing Group, 2007. (MS)

Shone, Rob. *Nelson Mandela: The Life of an African Statesman*. Illustrated by Neil Reed. Graphic Nonfiction Biographies Ser. New York: Rosen Publishing Group, 2007. (MS)

Shone, Rob. *Rosa Parks: The Life of a Civil Rights Heroine*. Illustrated by Nick Spender. Graphic Nonfiction Biographies Ser. New York: Rosen Publishing Group, 2007. (MS)

Shone, Rob, and Anita Generi. *Alexander the Great: The Life of a King and Conqueror*. Illustrated by Chris Odgers. Graphic Nonfiction Biographies Ser. New York: Rosen Publishing Group, 2007. (MS)

Resistance Series

Jablonski, Carla, Leland Purvis, and Hilary Sycamore. *Defiance: Resistance* Book 2. New York: First Second, 2011. (MS)

Jablonski, Carla, Leland Purvis, and Hilary Sycamore. *Resistance* Book 1. New York: First Second, 2010. (MS)

[§]Additional titles are available in the Graphic History Series.
[**]Additional titles are available in the Graphic Nonfiction Biographies Series.

Treasury of Victorian Murder[††]

Geary, Rick. *The Beast of Chicago.* New York: NBM, 2004. (HS)

Geary, Rick. *The Borden Tragedy: A Memoir of the Infamous Double Murder at Fall River, Mass., 1892.* New York: NBM, 1997. (HS)

Geary, Rick. *The Fatal Bullet: A True Account of the Assassination, Lingering Pain, Death, and Burial of James A. Garfield, Twentieth President of the United States.* New York: NBM, (1999) (HS)

Geary, Rick. *Jack the Ripper: A journal of the Whitechapel murders 1888–1889.* New York: NBM ComicsLit, 1995. (HS)

Geary, Rick. *The murder of Abraham Lincoln: a chronicle of 62 days in the life of the American Republic, March 4–May 4, 1865.* New York: NBM ComicsLit., 2005. (HS)

Graphic American History Series[‡‡]

The Civil Rights Movement & Vietnam 1960–1976. Irvine, CA: Saddleback Educational Pub., 2009. (MS)

The Civil War: 1850–1876. Irvine, CA: Saddleback Educational Pub., 2009. (MS)

The Fight for Freedom 1750–1783. Irvine, CA: Saddleback Educational Pub., 2009. (MS)

The Roaring Twenties & the Great Depression 1920–1940. Irvine, CA: Saddleback Educational Pub., 2009. (MS)

World War II & the Cold War 1940–1960. Irvine, CA: Saddleback Educational Pub., 2009. (MS)

Lesson Plans

Lesson Plan Title: The Battle of Gettysburg: A House Divided

Grade Level: MS

Subject Areas: Social Studies, U.S. History

Curriculum Focus/Concepts: Civil War, comparing and contrasting, primary and secondary resources

Graphic Novel Tie-In:
These three graphic novels cover the same topic for the same age student but are diverse in approach, focus, and style. The use of multiple resources strengthens a lesson in comparing and contrasting, and allows for differentiated instruction.

The Battle of Gettysburg by O'Hern, Anderson, and McHargue gives an overview of the Civil War battle. Information is factual and basic, and is organized simply and logically. The book covers the major causes of the war, important events of the battle, and a little of the aftermath, but without confusing detail. Broadly stylized art in bold colors makes the illustrations easy to follow and understand, immersing the reader in the action without focusing too much on individual characters. The book contains a list of additional resources for further reading.

[††]Additional titles are available in the Treasury of Victorian Murder Series.
[‡‡]Additional titles are available in the *Graphic American History* Series.

Pages like this from *The Battle of Gettysburg* (O'Hern & Anderson, 2006) help students visualize the challenges of war.

The Battle of Gettysburg: Spilled Blood on Sacred Ground by Abnett and Verma describes the events of the battle in greater detail. It focuses on the decisions of the commanders and maneuvers of the troops. Smaller panels in full color contain more realistic action, depicting the determination and desperation of the soldiers and their leaders. There is a great deal of dialogue, much of it in actual quotes. At the front of the book is information about the important commanders and at the end an aftermath, a glossary, a "further reading" section, and an index.

Gettysburg: The Graphic Novel by Butzer focuses more on the big picture—the numbers of soldiers involved, the dead, the horrors of battle from individual soldiers' perspectives, and what happened after the battle. The art is in shades of black, white, blue, and gray, with differing sizes of panels depending on the scope of the scene being portrayed. Actual battle scenes fill only fourteen pages of the book. The remainder describes what happened afterward: photographer Timothy O'Sullivan taking pictures of the dead, Pennsylvania Governor Curtin requesting a memorial and National Cemetery, and the famous speeches by Edward Everett and Abraham Lincoln during the memorial service. The action of the book ends with a stylized interpretation of The Gettysburg Address, with hints of struggles to come as Americans continue to fight for their freedoms. The book contains a cast of characters, author's notes, endnotes, and additional resources. The author brings his point of view to the story, lending itself to a discussion of primary versus secondary sources and historical perspective.

Objectives:
Students will trace the causes and effects of the Battle of Gettysburg.
Students will evaluate the Civil War from different perspectives and analyze how perspective influences viewpoint.

Students will understand the military campaigns of the Civil War.
Students will understand how ideas are expressed through artwork and point of view.
Students will analyze two or more texts to compare and contrast each author's approach and purpose.

Materials/Resources:
Books
The Battle of Gettysburg by Kerri O'Hern, Dale Anderson, and D. McHargue (World Almanac Library, 2006).
The Battle of Gettysburg: Spilled Blood on Sacred Ground by Dan Abnett (Rosen, 2007).
Gettysburg: The Graphic Novel by C. M. Butzer (Collins, 2009).
Gettysburg: the Bloodiest Battle of the Civil War by Jennifer Johnson (Franklin Watts, 2010).
Summer's Bloodiest Days: the Battle of Gettysburg as Told From All Sides by Jennifer Weber (National Geographic, 2010).

Websites
The Library of Congress's Civil War Photographs: http://memory.loc.gov/ammem/cwphtml/cwphome.html
http://memory.loc.gov/cgi-bin/query/v?ammem/cwar:0185-0209:T11

Procedures/Activities:
Teach about the Battle of Gettysburg as part of a unit on the Civil War, using the books and websites listed above, or your own resources.
Have students read parts or all of the three graphic novels about the battle.
Working as a whole class or in smaller groups, have students compare and contrast the three books, listing their differences and similarities, using a graphic organizer or chart.
Help students analyze the authors' approach and purpose; why they might have chosen the styles they did, what they wanted their readers to learn, how each author's point of view comes through in his or her story.
Show the photos on the Library of Congress's website.
Discuss primary and secondary sources and historical perspective.
Have students create a timeline of the events of the Battle of Gettysburg and its aftermath, including Lincoln's Gettysburg Address.

Discussion Questions:
Why was the Battle of Gettysburg a turning point in the Civil War?
What mistakes did both commanders make during the battle?
Why do we still read Lincoln's Gettysburg Address today?
What are the strengths and limitations of primary and secondary sources? Why do good researchers use both?
How does the artwork in the graphic novels reflect the topic?
How does each artist's medium and style make the art interdependent with the text?

Closure:
The Civil War is unlike any other war in American history. Discuss with students how the Battle of Gettysburg fit into the larger scope of the Civil War and the final toll, in loss of lives.

Extension Activities:
Take a virtual field trip to The Gettysburg National Military Park Museum: http://www.nps.gov/gett/
Have students conduct research on important people and events of the Civil War, with an understanding of the causes and effects of the Civil War.

Assessment:
Assess students' participation in the compare and contrast discussion, and creation of the timeline.

Lesson Plan Title: The Little Rock Nine

Grade Level: HS

Subject Areas: Social Studies, U.S. History

Curriculum Focus/Concepts: Civil rights, segregation, events of the twentieth century, primary and secondary resources

Graphic Novel Tie-In:
   Little Rock Nine, by Marshall Poe and Ellen Lindner, is a fictionalized account of the events in Little Rock, Arkansas during school desegregation, as seen through the eyes of two teen boys and their families. When used with information about the court case that led to integration and photos of the people and events, the graphic novel will lead to a deeper understanding of the motivations and emotions of the people involved as the civil rights events took place. *Little Rock Nine* contains racial epithets that were common during the time, necessitating a discussion with students to put the language into context.
   The art in *Little Rock Nine* is reminiscent of a black and white television show, giving readers a feel for the time period. The detailed facial expressions and abundance of dialogue helps readers immerse themselves in the characters' actions and feelings. It presents a clear, linear depiction of the events as nine African-American students attempted to attend Little Rock High, along with the reactions of townspeople, the Arkansas governor, and the U.S. president.

Objectives:
Students will evaluate the effects of racial segregation on U.S. society.
Students will trace major events of the civil rights movement and discuss their impact.
Students will make connections between historic and contemporary issues.
Students will discuss ideas about courage and standing up for what they feel is right.

Materials/Resources:
Books
Little Rock Nine by Marshall Poe and Ellen Lindner (Aladdin, 2008)
Little Rock Nine: Struggle for Integration by Stephanie Fitzgerald (Compass Point, 2007)

Websites
National Park Service's website for Little Rock Central High School: http://www.nps.gov/chsc/index.htm (Note: the site also contains excellent lesson plans).

Procedures/Activities:
Teach students about the U.S. Court case *Brown vs. Board of Education*, which declared that "separate educational facilities are inherently unequal," using Fitzgerald's book or other resources.
Read all, or portions of, Poe and Lindner's *Little Rock Nine* graphic novel.
Show students the Little Rock Central High School National Historic site, with a narrative, photos, oral history interviews, and a timeline of events.
Have students carry out research on the important laws and court cases of the civil rights era: Jim Crow laws, *Brown vs. Board of Education of Topeka*, the Civil Rights Act of 1964, the 14th Amendment, the Voting Rights Act, and so on.
Students can write a paper, create a presentation, complete an oral report, or use a technology tool of their choice to report to other students in the class.

Discussion Questions:
What is courage?
Is it always easy to stand up for what you believe?
What is segregation? In what ways were segregated schools unequal?
What restrictions were there for African-Americans prior to the civil rights era?
What important decisions did the governor of Arkansas and the president of the United States have to make with regard to Little Rock Central High School? What factors influenced them?
Is your school integrated? What factors have an impact on who attends which school?
What controversial issues do we face today that may be seen differently 50 years from now?
How does the artwork in the graphic novel reflect its topic?
How does the artist's medium and style make it interdependent with the text?

Closure:
Decades later, many public schools continue to bus students for racial and economic integration and diversity, while others have become more segregated. Have students discuss the lasting impact of school desegregation and issues faced by students, school districts, and families.

Extension Activities:
For additional accounts of young people involved in the civil rights movement, read: Ruby Bridges's book *Through My Eyes* (Scholastic Press, 1999) for a first-hand account of a girl's school desegregation experience, *Marching for Freedom: Walk Together Children and Don't You Grow Weary* by Elizabeth Partridge (Viking Juvenile, 2009) for a look at children who marched with Martin Luther King, Jr., in the March to Montgomery, and/or *Claudette Colvin: Twice Toward Justice* by Phillip Hoose (Melanie Kroupa Books, 2009) for a fascinating story of bus segregation.

Assessment:
Assess students' research and projects.

Chapter 15

Vote Yes!: Using Graphic Novels to Teach Political Science

Introduction

Face it . . . political science is not always the easiest subject to teach, and books about political science often collect dust on library shelves. Not anymore! Because they can make complicated issues more accessible to students, graphic novels are an attractive medium through which twenty-first century students can learn about political science. They can attract readers who may not have indicated any prior interest in reading books dealing with political science issues. Furthermore, many educators believe that graphic novels can facilitate student learning more effectively than through the use of traditional textbooks. As Schwarz (2002) writes, "Graphic novels can bring new life beyond bland textbooks" (p. 2). The captivating illustrations in graphic novels also allow for differentiated instruction by clarifying difficult topics such as political science to a variety of learners. For these, and reasons previously described in this book, graphic novels make excellent resources for supplementing the political science curriculum.

References

Schwarz, G. E. (2002). Graphic Novels for Multiple Literacies. *Journal of Adolescent & Adult Literacy, 46*(3), 262–65.

Connecting to the Standards

AASL Standards for the 21st-Century Learner

3.1.5 Connect learning to community issues.
3.3.3 Use knowledge and information skills and dispositions to engage in public conversation and debate around issues of common concern.

The Bottom Line

Elections, the atomic bomb, and immigration are all difficult political issues for middle and high school students to tackle. Reader-friendly texts such as graphic novels offer an additional approach for teaching students how to become engaged citizens.

3.3.6 Use information and knowledge in the service of democratic values.

4.1.3 Respond to literature and creative expressions of ideas in various formats and genres.

National Standards for History

Historical Thinking Standard 3 The student engages in historical analysis and interpretation.

Comic Connections

- To help middle school students understand the electoral process, use some of the titles from the Cartoon Nation Series by Capstone (listed below) to cover topics such as political parties, political elections, and how women obtained the right to vote.
- As part of a high school unit on the use of the atomic bomb in World War II, share some, or all, of the book *Fallout: J. Robert Oppenheimer, Leo Szilard, and the Political Science of the Atomic Bomb* with students (Ottaviani, 2001). Discuss the making of the bomb and its political implications. Have them read the following speech by President Harry Truman, that was made hours after the bomb was dropped at Hiroshima. www.learnnc.org/lp/editions/nchist -worldwar/5961.

Suggested Titles by Middle and High School (MS & HS)

Ottaviani, Jim. *Fallout: J. Robert Oppenheimer, Leo Szilard, and the Political Science of the Atomic Bomb.* Ann Arbor, MI: G.T. Labs, 2001. (HS)

Pekar, Harvey, Gary Dumm, and Paul Buhle. *Students for a Democratic Society: A Graphic History.* New York: Hill and Wang, 2008. (HS)

Tan, Shaun. *The Arrival.* New York: Arthur A. Levine Books, 2007. (MS & HS)

Suggested Titles in a Series (MS)

Cartoon Nation Series

Burgan, Michael, and Charles Barnett. *Political Parties.* Cartoon Nation Ser. Mankato, MN: Capstone Press, 2008. (MS)

Collins, Terry, and Brian Bascle. *Women's Right to Vote.* Cartoon Nation Ser. Mankato, MN: Capstone Press, 2009. (MS)

Miller, Davis, Katherine M. L. Brevard, and Charles Barnett. *Political Elections.* Cartoon Nation Ser. Mankato, MN: Capstone Press, 2008. (MS)

O'Donnell, Liam, and Charles Barnett. *U.S. Immigration*. Cartoon Nation Ser. Mankato, MN: Capstone Press, 2009. (MS)

Peterson, Christine and Bascle, Brian. *The U.S. Constitution. Cartoon Nation Series*. Mankato, MN: Capstone Press. (MS)

Skog, Jason. *Citizenship*. Cartoon Nation Ser. Mankato, MN: Capstone Press, 2008. (MS)

Lesson Plans

Lesson Plan Title: The U.S. Constitution

Grade Level: MS

Subject Areas: Political Science, Social Studies, U.S. History

Curriculum Focus/Concepts: U.S. government, founding fathers, Constitution Day political freedom, primary resources

Graphic Novel Tie-In:

September 17 is Constitution Day, a federally mandated holiday that celebrates the signing of the U.S. Constitution in 1787. All schools that receive federal funding must provide students with instruction about the Constitution on that day. This lesson is geared toward younger students, but use of major portions of Hennessey and McConnell's excellent graphic novel can be utilized with older students to delve into all parts of the Constitution.

The United States Constitution: A Graphic Adaptation, by Jonathan Hennessey and Aaron McConnell, covers the Constitution from beginning to end: the preamble, the seven articles, and all twenty-seven amendments. It contains easy-to-read panels, clear narration and voice bubbles, and clever symbolism. Both the Founding Fathers and more contemporary figures are clearly identifiable, and the information breaks the Constitution down into logical and easily understood parts.

Objectives:

Students will understand the foundations of American government, and why the Constitution was written.

Students will learn the significance of the U.S. Constitution and its impact on America's formation.

Students will make connections between historic and contemporary issues.

Materials/Resources:

Books

Aloian, Molly. *Constitution Day*. New York: Crabtree, 2009. (MS)

Hennessey, Jonathan and McConnell, Aaron. *The United States Constitution: A Graphic Adaptation*. New York: Hill & Wang, 2008. (MS & HS)

Peterson, Christine and Bascle, Brian. *The U.S. Constitution. Cartoon Nation Series*. Mankato, MN: Capstone Press, 2009 (MS)

Websites
National Archives' website with photos of the original Constitution of the United States: http://www.archives.gov/exhibits/charters/constitution.html

Procedures/Activities:
Have students view and read through the Preamble to the Constitution on the National Archive's site.
Create a glossary of unfamiliar terms and their definitions.
Project or share pages 2–5, 15, 18–22, and 25–26 of *The United States Constitution: A Graphic Adaptation* for information on the Constitution's Preamble.
Read parts of Aloian's *Constitution Day* for ideas of ways to celebrate the holiday.
Working in groups, have students put the preamble of the Constitution into modern-day language, or create a class constitution of classroom rules.
Help students brainstorm a list of ways your school could celebrate Constitution Day.

Discussion Questions:
Why did the Founding Fathers write the Constitution?
Why were the first three words of the Preamble written larger than the other words?
Why was the U.S. Constitution such a ground-breaking document?
How well has the Constitution stood the test of time?
Why do students celebrate Constitution Day?
How does the artwork in the graphic novel reflect its topic?
How does the artist's medium and style make it interdependent with the text?

Closure:
Have students discuss why a document like the U.S. Constitution, or a class constitution, is necessary for establishing justice, insuring domestic tranquility, providing for the common defense, promoting the general welfare, and securing the blessing of liberty.

Extension Activities:
If studying the Constitution in its entirety, use Macmillian's Teacher's Guide to *The United States Constitution: A Graphic Adaptation* for a more in-depth discussion of the book: http://media.us.macmillan.com/teachersguides/9780809094707TG.pdf.
Have students visit Constitutionfacts.com, a site that includes facts, games, puzzles, and ideas for celebrating Constitution Day: http://www.constitutionfacts.com/.
View the short video that shows how Aaron McConnell created the art for *The United States Constitution: A Graphic Adaptation:* http://us.macmillan.com/theunitedstates constitution

Assessment:
Assess the groups as they explain their contribution to the translation of the Preamble or class constitution, how they determined what was important, and how they came to an accord.

Lesson Plan Title: Journey to America—Immigration to the United States

Grade Level: HS

Subject Area: Political Science, Art

Curriculum Focus/Concepts: Social Studies, United States History, Immigration, Cultural Differences, Assimilation

Graphic Novel Tie-In:

The Arrival wordlessly tells the story of an immigrant who leaves his family to settle in a confusing new land. The main character, along with the reader, is thrown into a strange new world where kind strangers assist him along the way, as he makes this new place his home. Although told only in pictures, *The Arrival* uses symbolism and unique imagery in a way that gives the story depth and emotion, making it a good choice for use with high school students. Because it does not include text, it is also an excellent resource to use with immigrant students who are not native English speakers. They are certain to relate to the difficulties of the main character as he learns to live in his adopted land.

Objectives:

Students will develop an understanding of the lives of immigrants and the issues they face in adjusting to life in a new country.

Students will develop an understanding of some of the historical trends that have occurred in patterns of immigration to America.

Students will develop an understanding of the reasons immigrants come to the United States, and the effects of immigration on U.S. society.

Materials/Resources:
Books
Tan, Shaun. *The Arrival*. New York: Arthur A. Levine Books, 2007.
Hay, Jeff. *Immigration*. San Diego, CA: Greenhaven Press, 2001.
Say, Allen. *Grandfather's Journey*. Boston, MA: Houghton Mifflin, 1993.

Websites
Curriculum materials about Ellis Island for Grades 9–12 (National Park Service) http://www.nps.gov/elis/forteachers/materials-for-9th-grade-through-12th-grade.htm
The Immigrant Experience Website (Statue of Liberty and Ellis Island Foundation) http://www.ellisisland.org/Immexp/index.asp
Immigration: Stories of Yesterday and Today http://teacher.scholastic.com/activities/immigration/index.htm
The New Americans Website (PBS): http://www.pbs.org/independentlens/newamericans/foreducators.html (The site also contains excellent lesson plans on immigration.)
Personal Stories of Immigrants (PBS) http://www.pbs.org/destinationamerica/ps.html

Procedures/Activities:

Using the websites and other resources, provide background information regarding the immigration experience, the reasons people immigrate, and the ways that Americans respond to immigration.

Using a document camera, share some of the pages from *The Arrival* that show the central character when he first arrives in his new country.

- Have students describe the central character's first impressions of his new country.
- Ask them to discuss whether or not the small and larger pages of pictures, the color / shading, etc. are effective in telling the story?

Share some of the personal stories of immigrants available on the previous websites. Remind the students that immigration has been a controversial topic throughout the history of the United States. Provide examples by sharing the following quotes:

Everywhere immigrants have enriched and strengthened the fabric of American life.

—John F. Kennedy

Unless the stream of these people can be turned away from their country to other countries, they will soon outnumber us so that we will not be able to save our language or our government.

—Benjamin Franklin

Give me your tired, your poor,
Your huddled masses yearning to breathe free,
The wretched refuse of your teeming shore.
Send these, the homeless, tempest-tost to me,
I lift my lamp beside the golden door!

—Emma Lazarus
(inscribed on the Statue of Liberty)

Have students describe their reactions to these quotes, as well as their impressions of *The Arrival*, through class discussions or a written essay. Use the following discussion questions/writing prompts.

Discussion Questions/Writing prompts:

Why have people immigrated to the United States in the past? Why do people immigrate to the United States today?

Are there students in your school who have immigrated to the United States? If so, what do you think it is like for them? (If some of your students have immigrated, see if they are willing to share their experiences.)

What are some of the advantages and disadvantages for immigrants, and for the United States, when people from other lands settle here?

What are some of the issues that often develop for immigrants and for the United States?

How does the artwork in the graphic novel reflect its topic?

How does each artist's medium and style make the art interdependent with the text?

Closure:

Closing class discussion: There are many political, social, and ethical issues that make immigration the burning issue that it is today. After learning what you have through our unit on immigration, respond to the following question:

Do you think that the United States should allow anyone to immigrate here, or should there be a quota / limit on how many people come here from other countries? Justify your answers.

Extension Activities: Read, or project the picture book, *Grandfather's Journey* to the students. Have students describe the character's first impressions of his new country. Ask them to discuss whether or not the pictures, color/shading, and so on are effective in telling the story. Have students compare and contrast the two books, either orally or through a written activity.

Tell the students to pretend that they are a teenage immigrant arriving in America for the first time. Ask them to write a letter to their best friend back in their native country. Tell them to describe their journey to America, as well as their reactions when they first got off the boat at Ellis Island.

Assessment:

Assess the students' work through the use of a rubric.

Chapter 16

Nonstandard Deviation: Math Plus Graphic Novels

Introduction

Few graphic novels have been written that focus on math, but that doesn't mean graphic novels on all topics can't be used creatively to teach and reinforce math skills essential to middle and high school. Innovative math teachers have always tried to use interesting resources as their students count, graph, predict, perform computations, use probability, and solve equations. Math and comic art have many elements in common—patterns, proportions, shapes, symbols, and sequences—and panels can break complex topics into simpler steps. Graphic novels give teachers a resource that will motivate and appeal to math students.

Math topics are no different from other subjects when it comes to the power of visuals that comics offer. Gene Yang, author of several graphic novels including the 2007 Printz Award winner *American Born Chinese* (2006), is a high school math and computer science teacher. Years ago, he began drawing his math lessons in a comics format as a highly visual, self-paced guide to reinforce and reteach algebra skills to his students (Yang, 2008), and he created a web tutorial called "Factoring With Mr. Yang and Mosley the Alien: Webcomics Lessons for Algebra Students" (Yang, 2003) that breaks the advanced topic of factoring into clear sequential steps.

Good math skills are essential for understanding the world, logically solving problems, and succeeding in nearly every career choice. More graphic novels should be written that show adolescents how math is used in their daily lives. Perhaps you and your students can create comics of your own to illustrate practical uses for math, and to teach ratios, number lines, patterns, geometric shapes, and more.

References

Yang, Gene Leun. "Comics in Education." 2003. http://www.humblecomics.com/comicsedu/ (accessed Jan. 25, 2011).

Yang, Gene Leun. "Factoring With Mr. Yang and Mosley the Alien." 2003. http://www.humblecomics.com/factoring/ (accessed Jan. 25, 2011).

The Bottom Line

Graphic novels on math topics can help students break difficult concepts down into more easily understood parts.

Connecting to the Standards

AASL Standards for the 21st-Century Learner

2.1.3 Use strategies to draw conclusions from information and apply knowledge to curricular areas, real-world situations, and further investigations.

Suggested Titles by Middle and High School (MS & HS)

Doxiadis, Apostolos, and Christos Papadimitriou. *Logicomix: an Epic Search for Truth*. New York: Bloomsbury, 2009. (HS)

Gonick, Larry, and Woolcott Smith. *The Cartoon Guide to Statistics*. New York: Harper Perennial, 1993. (HS)

Yang, Gene Leun. *Prime Baby*. New York: First Second, 2010. (MS)

Suggested Titles in a Series

Manga Guides

Kojima, Hiroyuki. *The Manga Guide to Calculus*. Manga Guide Ser. San Francisco: No Starch Press, 2009. (HS)

Takahashi, Mana-Ohmsha. *Manga Guide to Databases*. Manga Guide Ser. San Francisco: No Starch Press, 2009. (HS)

Takahashi, Shin. *The Manga Guide to Statistics*. Manga Guide Ser. San Francisco: No Starch Press, 2009. (HS)

Lesson Plans

Lesson Plan Title: Coordinate Plane Comics

Grade Level: MS

Subject Area: Mathematics

Curriculum Focus/Concepts: Geometry, numbers and operations, graphing coordinate pairs

Graphic Novel Tie-In:

Understanding the coordinate plane, quadrants, and how to plot ordered pairs are important math skills for middle school students to master before moving on to graphing functions in algebra. Practice is required, as with all math skills, to create a foundation of understanding. Graphic novels can add a motivating factor when practicing for proficiency.

When young, most students probably enjoyed completing connect-the-dot pictures. These kinds of pictures are easily constructed on a coordinate plane. By using comic characters or panels as the theme of the lesson, students will enjoy artistically generating their own connect-the-dot pictures, and then having classmates complete the pictures by plotting the ordered pairs. Each student can create his or her own picture, color it, and list the ordered pairs necessary for other students to complete the pictures on their own.

Objectives:
Students will demonstrate an understanding of the coordinate plane.
Students will follow step-by-step directions to solve problems.
Students will graph ordered pairs on a coordinate plane.
Students will apply information about the coordinate plane to real-life experiences.
Students will learn about the connection between mathematics and art.

Materials/Resources:
Books
One graphic novel per student, or comic panels obtained by students. Panels can be enlarged in order to fit better on a standard sheet of graph paper.

Materials
Graph paper, markers, colored pencils, crayons

Procedures/Activities:
Teach students about x- and y-axis, the coordinate plane, quadrants, and plotting ordered pairs.
Explain that students will choose a comic panel to draw or trace onto graph paper with x- and y-axis drawn in the center. They will then choose points on the drawing that will be the basis of their connect-the-dots picture.
Have students create a list of ordered pairs that show where their chosen points are located.
Require students to use a minimum of a specific number of ordered pairs.
Have students color their comics once they have plotted all the points and connected the points as needed.
For other students to solve the dot-to-dot pictures on their own, have them graph the points and connect the dots with line segments.

Discussion Questions:
What vocabulary words are important to know in order to understand the coordinate plane?
What happens if you are careless when listing your ordered pairs?
What careers might utilize graphing points on a coordinate plane to create art (graphic design, animation, map-making)?

Closure:
Have students complete one another's connect-the-dot pictures (without seeing the picture) by plotting the ordered pairs. Display the colored pages.

Extension Activities:
Have students create similar drawings in a computer lab with one of the free graphing games available online, or with Adobe Photoshop Elements.

Assessment:
Assess students' drawings and lists of ordered pairs as assigned by the teacher.

Lesson Plan Title: Ratio and Scale Factor

Grade Level: MS, HS

Subject Area: Mathematics

Curriculum Focus/Concepts: Measurement, geometry, ratios, proportion, scale factor

Graphic Novel Tie-In:
Variations of this math/art lesson are frequently used by teachers. The activity helps students understand scale factor, and is a great method for enlarging drawings without using photocopiers or scanners. Not only is it a fun way to teach these concepts, but it can be used in other subject areas when it is necessary to enlarge a comic panel.

Using comics as a part of math lessons engages students. Even those who believe they lack artistic skills will be able to draw a larger version of a panel with this method, because there is no talent required, just the ability to copy what is in a grid.

Objectives:
Students will understand and use measurement, ratios, and proportions.
Students will apply information about ratio and proportion to real-life situations.
Students will utilize scale factors to enlarge a drawing.
Students will learn about the connection between mathematics and art.

Materials/Resources:
Books
One graphic novel per student, or comic panels obtained by students

Materials
Rulers, paper, pencils, markers, colored pencils, construction paper

Procedures/Activities:
Teach students about ratios and scale factors.
Have students bring in a comic panel from the newspaper, or find a panel they like in a graphic novel. If the panel is from a book, make a photocopy of it.

Have students draw a square grid on the comic panel, with lines every centimeter. See pictures for examples. They may trim the picture as needed, so that all blocks in the grid are 1 cm by 1 cm.

Tell students to measure the length of one side of the comic, then enlarge the comic by a scale factor of 2, 3, or 4. For example, if the comic is small, they might decide the scale factor should be 1 cm = 4 cm. Students can determine scale factor like this:

This bulletin board contains math-related graphic novel assignments.

$$\text{Scale Factor} = \frac{\text{Length of your larger drawing}}{\text{Length of the original comic}}$$

Have students draw the enlarged square grid on a sheet of paper. They then will carefully fill in each square, one by one, with exactly what they see in the corresponding, smaller square of the original comic.

Once they are finished, students should color their enlarged panels to look like the originals.

Have students glue both the original and their drawing to a sheet of construction paper and include the scale factor they used, in its simplest form.

Discussion Questions:
How are scale factor, ratio, and proportion related?
What happened if you were careless when drawing your grid or transferring your comic?
What careers might utilize ratios, proportions, and scale drawings (graphic design, architecture, video game design, illustrator, animation, map-making)?
In what other ways are ratios and proportions applicable to real-life situations?

Closure:
Hang the finished projects on the wall to display them, and have students do a gallery walk.

Extension Activities:
Have students draw to-scale floor plans of their bedrooms and cut out pieces of paper that represent their large pieces of furniture. Then, have students find a different way to place their furniture for a new look.

Examples of ratio and scale factor are made through the use of graphic novels and graphing paper.

Assessment:
Assess students' drawings and make certain instructions were followed.

Lesson Plan Title:
Calculus Comics

Grade Level: HS

Subject Areas: Mathematics, Calculus

Curriculum Focus/Concepts: Functions, derivatives, differentiation, integration

Graphic Novel Tie-In:

The Manga Guide to Calculus, by Hiroyuki Kojima, a translation of the Japanese EduManga book, connects calculus to real life situations involving economics, physics, and science. With an interesting format that includes characters in the popular style of manga, this rigorous book does an excellent job of taking concepts from calculus—from basic to complex—and giving everyday examples of their uses. Concepts typically difficult to visualize are broken down and explained clearly, making them easier to understand and allowing students to build from the early basic concepts of calculus to the later compound processes.

This book can be used as an engaging introduction to new concepts followed by examples that will further students' understanding. The actual formulas are included in variable form, with problems for students to work through numerically.

Objectives:
Students will develop an understanding of functions.
Students will use derivatives to solve problems.
Students will use integrals to solve problems.
Students will use calculus to solve real-world problems.

Materials/Resources:
Books
Kojima, Hiroyuki. *The Manga Guide to Calculus.* San Francisco: No Starch Press, 2009.

Materials
Paper, markers, colored pencils

Procedures/Activities:
Project or share portions of the book to introduce new concepts in calculus such as: functions, differentiation, derivatives, integrals, Taylor expansions, and partial derivatives.
Use the story lines to show students how to visualize a concept, learn it, and follow the step-by-step methods to solve problems using the formulas.
Once a concept has been covered, have students practice for further understanding by creating their own graphic panels that illustrate that concept.
Students should draw their comic panels by crafting real-life problems that can be solved using calculus, using examples in the book as models.

Discussion Questions:
How do graphic panels help break concepts down when covering a complex topic like calculus?
What does the graphic novel have in common with your textbook? What is different?
How does an understanding of ways to use calculus in real life make it easier to learn?

Closure:
Have students read one another's problems and solve them.

Extension Activities:
Discuss with the class Noriko's assertion that the purpose of mathematics is "to convey things that cannot be conveyed in words" (p. 224).

Assessment:
Assess students' graphic panels, and how well their problems reflected the concepts and were applicable to real-life situations.

Chapter 17

Picture This: Teaching Fine Arts with Graphic Novels

Introduction

There are graphic novels that touch on different topics within the arts—visual arts, music, dance, movies, photography, cooking—but the easiest way to tie graphic novels into arts education is to study the remarkable artwork within the books. Nearly every style of art imaginable can be found in graphic novels, from realistic to abstract, delicate to bold, and colorful to stark. Some graphic novels even contain mixed media, like Emmanuel Guibert's award-winning book *The Photographer: Into War-Torn Afghanistan With Doctors Without Borders* (First Second, 2009), which includes photos among the comic panels.

Computer programs are available for art students who are interested in comic design. The simplest are comic creators, and free online programs are readily available (http://www.makebeliefscomix.com/, http://marvel.com/games/play/34/create _your_own_comic, http://www.readwritethink.org/files/resources/interactives/ comic/). These tools allow students to add pre-selected characters, backgrounds, and props to comic panels, then customize them by changing details and colors, and adding text. More serious comic art students can sketch comics and scan them into a computer, or draw them directly onto a computer using a graphics tablet with a pen-like stylus. Once the drawing is digitized, software like Photoshop can be utilized to create layers to the work. Heavier lines can be inked, colors can be filled in perfectly, and panels, speech bubbles, and text can be added—all with professional looking results. By using these digital tools, students can produce polished comics that reflect their own talent and creativity.

No study of movies and filmmaking is complete without a discussion of graphic novel tie-ins. Dozens of movies have been made from graphic novels and comics, and techniques used in movie storyboarding are similar to those involved in creating comics. Storyboards are, essentially, comic panels showing the placement of characters, their costumes, and the action taking place in a scene. Many moviemakers, especially those making animated films, painstakingly create storyboards of scenes before any filming takes place. Students interested in moviemaking will enjoy creating storyboards as part of the process of creating films.

Why does the public pour in to see movies like *The Dark Knight*? For the same reasons they are attracted to the comic books and graphic novels on which these movies are based: action-packed plots, compelling settings, and characters struggling with issues of good versus evil. These are some American movies that began as comics and graphic novels:

- *Batman* series
- *The Dark Knight*
- *Fantastic Four*
- *Spider-Man* series
- *Josie and the Pussycats*
- *The Mask*
- *The Incredible Hulk*
- *X-Men* series
- *Road to Perdition*
- *Sin City*
- *Superman* series
- *Iron Man*
- *V for Vendetta*
- *300*
- *Hellboy*
- *Alien vs. Predator*
- *Men in Black*
- *Time Cop*
- *Fantastic Four*
- *Dick Tracy*
- *The Crow*
- *League of Extraordinary Gentlemen*
- *Scott Pilgrim*
- *Watchmen*
- *Unbreakable*
- *Blade*
- *Catwoman*
- *Kick-Ass*
- *The Green Hornet*
- *Jonah Hex*
- *Cowboys and Aliens*
- *Green Lantern*
- *Thor*
- *Captain America*
- *Red*

Connecting to the Standards

AASL Standards for the 21st-Century Learner

4.1.8 Use creative and artistic formats to express personal learning.

National Standards for Arts Education

Visual Art Standard 5: Content Standard: Reflecting on and assessing the characteristics and merits of their work and the work of others.

Comic Connections

- Use *To Dance: A Ballerina's Graphic Novel* by Siena Cherson Siegel and Mark Seigel, for middle school, and *Isadora Duncan: A Graphic Biography* by Sabrina Jones, for high school, with dance students. Have them compare the main characters' dreams and training with their own.
- Use the short, one-page comics in Kazu Kibuishi's *Copper* to

teach the elements of comics and the creative use of color and panel shapes. In a chapter on comic design at the end of his book, Kibuishi explains how he draws, pencils, letters, and inks by hand, and then uses technology to add layers of color.

- Have students compare a graphic novel with its movie.
- Using pages 112 through 123 of Jim McCann and Janet Lee's *Return of the Dapper Men*, lead students in a discussion of artists' style, showing how illustrations of the same characters and setting differ according to the artists' interpretations.

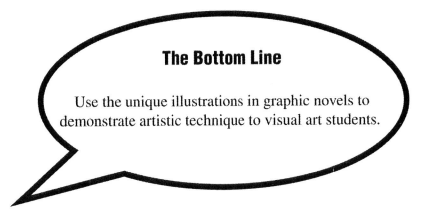

The Bottom Line

Use the unique illustrations in graphic novels to demonstrate artistic technique to visual art students.

Suggested Titles by Middle and High School (MS & HS)

Gipi. *Garage Band*. New York: First Second, 2007. (HS)

Guibert, Emmanuel. *The Photographer: Into War-Torn Afghanistan With Doctors Without Borders*. New York: First Second, 2009. (HS)

Ishihara, Yoko. *The Manga Cookbook*. Saitama, Japan: Japanime Co., 2007. (MS)

Jones, Sabrina. *Isadora Duncan: A Graphic Biography*. New York: Hill and Wang, 2008. (HS)

Kibuishi, Kazu. *Copper*. New York: Graphix, 2010. (MS)

Kleist, Reinhard. *Johnny Cash: I See Darkness: A Graphic Novel*. New York: Abrams ComicArts 2009. (HS)

McCann, Jim and Janet Lee. *Return of the Dapper Men*. Los Angeles, CA: Archaia Comics, 2010. (MS)

O'Hern, Kerri. *Louis Armstrong*. New York: World Almanac, 2007. (MS)

Siegel, Siena Cherson. *To Dance: A Ballerina's Graphic Novel*. New York: Atheneum Books for Young Readers, 2006. (MS)

Suggested Titles in a Series

Kobayashi, Miyuki. *Kitchen Princess* Series. New York: Del Ray/Ballentine. (MS & HS)

Lesson Plans

Lesson Plan Title: Sidewalk Paintings Lichtenstein Style

Grade Level: MS, HS

Subject Areas: Visual Arts, Art History

Curriculum Focus/Concepts: American art history, Pop Art, drawing, artistic technique, analysis of works of art

Graphic Novel Tie-In:

American artist Roy Lichtenstein changed the art world in 1961 when he began creating art that featured comics and advertisements. A trained artist and university professor, he experimented with the bold colors of comics and painted with dots, using techniques similar to those used by printers. Lichtenstein painted stylized pop culture images that were instantly understood, and often copied his images directly from comic books, altering the graphics based on his own observations and interpretation. His graphic art received immediate attention and over the years was hugely successful. This success led to other artists working with similar images and steered comics toward legitimacy they previously lacked.

Lichtenstein's art generated controversy—not only because of its basis in comics and advertisements, but because he used and modified the work of others. These issues can be examined to educate students in the basics of copyright and free use.

Objectives:
Students will understand and appreciate the art of Roy Lichtenstein.
Students will learn about the Pop Art movement in twentieth-century American art.
Students will discuss copyright and plagiarism issues produced by copying others' art.
Students will develop and explore their own talent as they create art.

Materials/Resources:
Books
A graphic novel for each student in the class

Websites
Biographical information about Roy Lichtenstein's life, including photos of his artwork, from the website of the Roy Lichtenstein Foundation at http://www.lichtenste infoundation.org/

Materials
High-quality art chalk, such as Prang Freart chalk, in assorted colors including black
A large space on the school's sidewalk to use for drawing graphic panels in chalk

Procedures/Activities:
Teach students about the life and ground-breaking art of Roy Lichtenstein.
Show students examples of his paintings.
Discuss how Lichtenstein used the work of others, and whether or not he would be able to do so today within copyright laws.
Have each student find a panel (or smaller portion of a panel) in a graphic novel to enlarge and draw.
Use the chalk to draw their interpretation of the panel on the sidewalk.
Students may use the ratio scale factor from the math lesson on page 134, with a grid of 3 squares by 3 squares. Students should draw the grid and large objects in white chalk, add color, and outline in black.
The finished square should be about 3 feet by 3 feet, large enough to have an impact on those viewing it.

Discussion Questions:
Why did Lichtenstein feature comics and ads in his art? What, and who, influenced him?
How did he change the originals to reflect his observations, intentions, and style?
Why did Lichtenstein's art generate controversy?
Do you think artists should be able to take the work of others and alter it? Could an artist today do the same thing?
What, to you, is appealing and unique about the art of Roy Lichtenstein?

After learning about the graphic artist Roy Lichtenstein, these students begin to create their own sidewalk art based on graphic novel panels.

Closure:
Have students compare the original panels from their graphic novels to their finished chalk drawings. How did their interpretations and style change the art? Is this similar to what Lichtenstein did?

Extension Activities:
Have students study other Pop Art artists such as Andy Warhol, James Rosenquist, Claes Oldenberg, and Jasper Johns.

Assessment:
Assess students' participation in the discussions and drawings, along with a "Gallery Walk" peer assessment by others in the class.

Lesson Plan Title: A Day in the Life

Grade Level: HS

Subject Areas: Visual Arts, English Language Arts, Film

Curriculum Focus/Concepts:
Drawing, personal technique, art careers

Students enjoy collaborating on their graphic novel art projects.

The final super product.

Graphic Novel Tie-In:

Just as art and text in high-quality graphic novels are interdependent, the best movies use many elements in tandem to tell a story: action, scenery, characters, costumes, dialogue, and music. Movies are expensive to make, and must be planned out carefully before the first scene is filmed. One way this is done is through the use of storyboards.

A storyboard is like a graphic representation of a movie. Graphic novels and storyboards have many similarities, and any student interested in drawing or moviemaking should be enthusiastic about putting together a storyboard. Adolescents are often narrowly focused on themselves, and creating a story about a day in their lives is an assignment they will find easy and interesting.

A short lesson about graphic novels and/or storyboards should be taught before beginning this lesson, with information about comic elements like panels, gutters, and voice bubbles. The lesson on page 48 of this book can be used. Instruct students to include different kinds of "shots" in their storyboards for added interest; wide angle shots that show all the action, and close ups that show the details of a scene.

Objectives:

Students will explore art techniques to communicate ideas.
Students will use critical thinking to develop ideas and images that tell a story.
Students will create a storyboard in panels.

Materials/Resources:

Examples of graphic representations of stories, such as graphic novels and film clips
Paper, pencils, colored pencils, markers, and other art supplies as needed

Procedures/Activities:

Have students examine graphic novels while listening to an introductory lesson on the format.
Discuss storyboards and how they are used in moviemaking. An excellent video on how storyboards were used by Disney and other filmmakers titled *Finding Lady: the Art of Storyboarding* can be found at http://video.google.com/videoplay?docid =-2412052664775629371&hl=en#.
Discuss moviemaking techniques such as close-ups, long shots and camera view.
Have students create a storyboard of one day in their lives. It can be a routine day or a special one, and should be developed with their own creativity and perspective.

Have students draw a specific number of scenes or panels and color them using their own technique and style.

Discussion Questions:
If using the storyboarding video:
How did storyboarding contribute to the success of Disney filmmaking?
How did Disney's success lead to storyboarding being used in live action films by later filmmakers?
Why are there few women employees in the clips from Disney studios? Do you think this is still true today?

Additional Questions:
How are storyboards and graphic novels similar? How are they different?
How do filmmaking techniques like close-ups and camera angles give a sense of style and perspective to a storyboard?

Closure:
Discuss why students chose specific days for their storyboards, and how they used certain techniques to show their own style.

Extension Activities:
Have students watch one of the movies discussed in the storyboarding video, examining it for techniques covered during the lesson.

Assessment:
Assess the students' projects based on a rubric.

Chapter 18

Coming of Age with Comics: Social Issues in Graphic Novels

Introduction

Librarians and teachers have long known the value of using books in therapeutic ways with students and patrons of all ages. Since ancient times, the library was considered the healing place of the soul (Galen and Johns, 1979). Bibliotherapy is defined as an attempt to use literature to help individuals understand themselves and to cope with problems relevant to their personal situations and developmental needs at the appropriate time (Hebert and Kent, 2000). There are a number of graphic novels available that can help middle and high school students address sensitive social issues such as divorce, bullying, eating disorders, and death. Working with guidance counselors and administrators, librarians and teachers can match students with graphic novels to help them address the issues that many adolescents experience. Furthermore, there are several coming of age graphic novels that portray adolescent characters learning a lesson and developing an understanding of themselves and others. Reading coming-of-age graphic novels can help adolescents realize that everyone has problems in life and may enable them to find solutions on their own.

References

Galen, Nancy and Johns, Jerry L. Children in Conflict. *School Library Journal. 26*(3), 25–30, 1979.
Hebert, Terry P. and Kent, Richard. Nurturing Social and Emotional Development in Gifted Teenagers through Young Adult Literature. *Roeper Review, 22*(3), 167–72, 2000.

Connecting to the Standards
AASL Standards for the 21st-Century Learner

4.3.3 Seek opportunities for pursuing personal and aesthetic growth.

The Bottom Line

For years, librarians and teachers have used books to help young adults deal with personal and social issues. Why not include graphic novels on these topics the next time you suggest titles to a student/patron, or their parents?

Comic Connections

- Guidance counselors are often the first faculty members that students turn to when they are experiencing challenging personal and social issues in their lives. However, it is unlikely that your guidance counselors are aware that there are graphic novels dealing with such issues. Gather some of the titles on this list and show them to your counselors, so that they can share them with students who approach them for help.

Suggested Titles for Middle and High School (MS & HS)

Bullying

Vachss, Andrew H., Frank T. Caruso, and Zak Mucha. *Heart Transplant*. Milwaukie, OR: Dark Horse, 2010. (HS)

Coming of Age Stories

Clugston, Chynna. *Queen Bee*. New York: Scholastic Graphix, 2005. (MS & HS)
Friedman, Aimee. *Breaking Up*. Illustrated by Christine Norrie. New York: Scholastic Graphix, 2007. (HS)
Gipi. *Garage Band*. New York: First Second Publishing, 2007. (HS) (Mature)
Larson, Hope. *Mercury*. New York: Athenuem Books, 2010. (HS)
Stuck in the Middle: 17 Comics from an Unpleasant Age. Schrag, Ariel (Ed.). New York: Viking Juvenile Publishing, 2007. (HS)
Tamaki, Mariko. *Skim*. Illustrated by Jillian Tamaki. Toronto, Ontario: Groundwood Books, 2008. (HS)
Telgemeier, Raina. *Smile*. New York: Scholastic Graphix, 2010. (MS)
Thompson, Craig. *Blankets*. Portland, OR: Top Shelf Productions, 2003. (HS)

Eating Disorders

Fairfield, Lesley. *Tyranny*. Plattsburgh, NY: Tundra Books, 2009. (HS)
Lasko-Gross, Miss. *Escape from Special*. Seattle, WA: Fantagraphics, 2006. (HS)
Lasko-Gross, Miss. *A Mess of Everything*. Seattle, WA: Fantagraphics, 2009. (HS)
Shivack, Nadia. *Inside Out: Portrait of an Eating Disorder*. New York: Ginee Seo Books, 2007. (HS)

Gangs

Canada, Geoffrey. *Fist Stick Knife Gun: A Personal History of Violence*. Boston, MA: Beacon Press, 2010. (HS)
Neri, G. *Yummy: The Last Days of a Southside Shorty*. Illustrated by Randy Duburke. New York: Lee & Low Books, 2010. (MS & HS)

Homelessness

Landowne, Youme. *Pitch Black.* Illustrated by Anthony Horton. El Paso, TX: Cinco Puntos Press, 2008. (HS)

Homosexuality

Winick, Judd. *Pedro and Me: Friendship, Loss, and What I Learned.* New York: Henry Holt & Company, 2009. (HS)

Mental Issues

White, Tracy. *How I Made It to Eighteen: A Mostly True Story.* New York: Roaring Brook Press, 2010. (HS) (Mature)

Sickness

Fies, Brian. *Mom's Cancer.* New York: Abrams Books, 2006. (MS & HS)
Small, David. *Stitches: A Memoir.* New York: W.W.Norton & Company, 2009. (HS)

War

Jablonski, Carla. *Resistance, Book 1.* Illustrated by Leland Purvis. New York: First Second Publishing, 2010. (MS & HS) (First title in the trilogy.)
Novgorodoff, Danica, James Ponsoldt, and Benjamin Percy. *Refresh, Refresh.* New York: First Second Publishing, 2009. (HS) (Mature)

Appendix 1

A Suggested Core List of Graphic Novel Titles for Middle School Students

Abadzis, Nick, and Hilary Sycamore. *Laika*. New York: First Second, 2007.

Arakawa, Hiromu. *Fullmetal Alchemist. Volume 1*. San Francisco, CA: Viz Media, LLC, 2006.

Arakawa, Hiromu. *Fullmetal Alchemist. Volume 2*. San Francisco, CA: Viz Media, LLC, 2006.

Arakawa, Hiromu. *Fullmetal Alchemist. Volume 3*. San Francisco, CA: Viz Media, LLC, 2006.

Arakawa, Hiromu. *Fullmetal Alchemist. Volume 4*. San Francisco, CA: Viz Media, LLC, 2006.

Arakawa, Hiromu. *Fullmetal Alchemist. Volume 5*. San Francisco, CA: Viz Media, LLC, 2006.

Bendis, Brian Michael, Mark Bagley, and Art Thibert. *Ultimate Spider-Man Vol. 2: Learning Curve*. New York: Marvel Comics, 2002.

Bendis, Brian Michael, Mark Bagley, and Art Thibert. *Ultimate Spider-Man Vol. 3: Double Trouble*. New York: Marvel Comics, 2001.

Bendis, Brian Michael, Mark Bagley, and Art Thibert. *Ultimate Spider-Man Vol. 4: Legacy*. New York: Marvel Comics, 2002.

Bendis, Brian Michael, Mark Bagley, and Art Thibert. *Ultimate Spider-Man Vol. 5: Public Scrutiny*. New York: Marvel Comics, 2002.

Burgan, Michael. *The Battle of Gettysburg*. Minneapolis, MN: Compass Point Books, 2001.

Busiek, Kurt, Alex Ross, and Richard Starkings. *Marvels*. New York: Marvel Publishing, 2008.

Chantler, Scott. *Tower of Treasure*. Toronto: Kids Can Press, 2010.

Colfer, Eoin, Andrew Donkin, Giovanni Rigano, and Paolo Lamanna. *Artemis Fowl: The Graphic Novel*. New York: Hyperion Books for Children, 2007.

Crilley, Mark. *Miki Falls: Spring*. New York, NY: Harper Teen, 2007.

Crilley, Mark. *Miki Falls: Summer*. New York: Harper Teen, 2007.

Crilley, Mark. *Miki Falls: Autumn*. New York: Harper Teen, 2007.

Crilley, Mark. *Miki Falls: Winter*. New York: Harper Teen, 2008.

Davis, Eleanor. *The Secret Science Alliance and the Copycat Crook*. New York: Bloomsbury, 2009. (MS)

Dembicki, Matt. *Trickster: Native American Tales: A Graphic Collection*. Golden, CO: Fulcrum Pub., 2010.

Deutsch, Barry. *Hereville: How Mirka Got Her Sword*. New York: Amulet, 2010.

Dixon, Chuck, David Wenzel, Sean Deming, and J. R. R. Tolkien. *The Hobbit: An Illustrated Edition of the Fantasy Classic*. New York: Ballantine Books, 2001.

Giffen, Keith, and John Rogers. *Blue Beetle: Shellshocked*. New York: DC Comics, 2006.

Hale, Shannon, Dean Hale, and Nathan Hale. *Rapunzel's Revenge*. New York: Bloomsbury, 2008.

Hamilton, Tim, and Ray Bradbury. *Ray Bradbury's Fahrenheit 451: The Authorized Adaptation.* New York: Hill and Wang, 2009.

Hennessey, Jonathan, and Aaron McConnell. *The United States Constitution: A Graphic Adaptation.* New York: Hill and Wang, 2008.

Heuvel, Eric, Ruud van der Rol, Lies Schippers, and Lorraine T. Miller. *The Search.* New York: Farrar, Straus and Giroux, 2009.

Hinds, Gareth. *The Odyssey: A Graphic Novel.* New York: Candlewick Press, 2010.

Horowitz, Anthony. *Stormbreaker.* New York: Philomel Books, 2001.

Horowitz, Anthony, Antony Johnston, Kanako Damerum, and Yuzuru Takasaki. *Point Blank: [the Graphic Novel].* New York: Philomel Books, 2007.

Jacobson, Sid, and Ernie Colon. *Anne Frank: The Anne Frank House Authorized Graphic Biography.* New York: Hill and Wang Publishing, 2010.

Jacobson, Sid, Ernie Colón, Thomas H. Kean, and Lee Hamilton. *The 9/11 Report: A Graphic Adaptation.* New York: Hill and Wang, 2006.

Jacques, Brian, Bret Blevins, Stuart Moore, and Richard Starkings. *Redwall: The Graphic Novel.* New York: Philomel Books, 2007.

Jemas, Bill, Brian M. Bendis, and Mark Bagley. *Ultimate Spider-Man Vol. 1: Power and Responsibility.* New York: Marvel Comics, 2002.

Kibuishi, Kazu. *Amulet: Book One The Stonekeeper.* New York: Graphix, 2008.

Kibuishi, Kazu. *Amulet: Book Two The Stonekeeper's Curse.* New York: Graphix, 2009.

Kibuishi, Kazu. *Amulet: Book Three The Cloud Searchers.* New York: Graphix, 2010.

Kim, Young, and Stephenie Meyer. *Twilight: The Graphic Novel.* New York: Yen Press, 2010.

Kneece, Mark, Rod Serling, and Anthony Spay. *Rod Serling's the Twilight Zone: The Midnight Sun.* New York: Walker & Co, 2009.

Kovac, Tommy, Lewis Carroll, and Sonny Liew. *Wonderland.* New York: Disney Press, 2008.

Kubo, Tite, Lance Caselman, and Joe Yamazaki. *Bleach 1: Strawberry and the Soul Reapers.* San Francisco, CA: Viz, 2004.

Kubo, Tite, Lance Caselman, and Joe Yamazaki. *Bleach 2: Goodbye Parakeet, Good Night My Sister.* San Francisco, CA: Viz, 2004.

Kubo, Tite, and Lance Caselman. *Bleach 3: Memories in the Rain.* San Francisco, CA: Viz, 2004.

Kubo, Tite, and Lance Caselman. *Bleach 4: Quincy Archer Hates You.* San Francisco, CA: Viz, 2004.

Kubo, Tite, and Lance Caselman. *Bleach 5: Right Arm of the Giant.* San Francisco, CA: Viz, 2006.

Lee, NaRae, James Patterson, and Abigail Blackman. *Maximum Ride: 1.* New York: Yen Press, 2009.

Lee, NaRae, James Patterson, and Abigail Blackman. *Maximum Ride: 2.* New York: Yen Press, 2009.

Lee, NaRae, James Patterson, and Abigail Blackman. *Maximum Ride: 3.* New York: Yen Press, 2010.

Lee, Tony, Sam Hart, and Artur Fujita. *Outlaw: The Legend of Robin Hood, a Graphic Novel.* Somerville, MA: Candlewick Press, 2009.

Lemke, Donald B., Tod Smith, and A. Milgrom. *Investigating the Scientific Method with Max Axiom, Super Scientist.* Mankato, MN: Capstone Press, 2008.

Loeb, Jeph, Tim Sale, and Bob Kane. *Batman: The Long Halloween.* New York: DC Comics, 1998.

Loeb, Jeph, and Tim Sale. *Superman for All Seasons.* New York: DC Comics, 1999.

Lutes, Jason, and Nick Bertozzi. *Houdini: The Handcuff King.* New York: Hyperion, 2007.

MacHale, D. J., and Carla S. McNeil. *Pendragon Graphic Novel: Book One.* New York: Aladdin Paperbacks, 2008.

McCann, Jim, and Janet Lee. *The Return of the Dapper Men.* Los Angeles: Archaia Comics, 2010.

McCloud, Scott. *Understanding Comics: The Invisible Art.* New York: Harper Perennial, 1994.

Millar, Mark, Adam Kubert, Andy, Kubert, and Art Thibert. *Ultimate X-Men: The Tomorrow People.* New York: Marvel Comics, 2001.

Neri, G. *Yummy: The Last Days of a Southside Shorty.* New York: Lee & Low Books, 2010.

O'Connor, George. *Zeus: King of the Gods.* New York: First Second, 2010.

Ottaviani, Jim, Zander Cannon, and Kevin Cannon. *T-minus: The Race to the Moon.* New York: Aladdin, 2009.

Phelan, Matt. *The Storm in the Barn.* Somerville, MA: Candlewick Press, 2009.

Poe, Edgar. *Nevermore: A Graphic Adaptation of Edgar Allan Poe's Short Stories.* New York: Sterling Publishing, 2008.

Poe, Marshall, and Ellen Lindner. *Little Rock Nine.* New York: Aladdin Paperbacks, 2008.

Renier, Aaron, and Alec Longstreth. *The Unsinkable Walker Bean.* New York: First Second, 2010.

Riordan, Rick, Robert Venditti, Attila Futaki, and Josè Villarrubia. *The Lightning Thief: the Graphic Novel.* New York: Disney/Hyperion Books, 2010.

Russell, P. C., Lovern Kindzierski, Todd Klein, and Neil Gaiman. *Coraline.* New York: HarperCollins, 2008.

Satrapi, Marjane. *Persepolis.* New York: Pantheon Books, 2003.

Shakespeare, William. *A Midsummer Night's Dream.* Adapted by Richard Appignanesi and illustrated by Kate Brown. Manga Shakespeare Ser. London: SelfMadeHero, 2008.

Shakespeare, William. *Romeo and Juliet.* Adapted by Richard Appignanesi and illustrated by Sonia Leong. Manga Shakespeare Ser. London: SelfMadeHero, 2007.

Shiga, Jason. *Meanwhile.* New York: Amulet Books, 2010.

Siddell, Tom. *Gunnerkrigg Court: Volume 1.* Fort Lee, NJ: Archaia Studios Press, 2008.

Siegel, Siena C., and Mark Siegel. *To Dance: A Memoir.* New York: Atheneum Books for Young Readers, 2006.

Smith, Jeff, and Steve Hamaker. *Bone: Out from Boneville.* New York: Graphix/Scholastic, 2005.

Smith, Jeff, and Steve Hamaker. *Bone: The Great Cow Race.* New York: Graphix/Scholastic, 2005.

Smith, Jeff, and Steve Hamaker. *Bone: Eyes of the Storm.* New York: Graphix/Scholastic, 2006.

Smith, Jeff, and Steve Hamaker. *Bone: The Dragon Slayer.* New York: Graphix/Scholastic, 2006.

Smith, Jeff, and Steve Hamaker. *Bone: Master of the Eastern Border.* New York: Graphix/Scholastic, 2007.

Smith, Jeff. *Shazam!: The Monster Society of Evil.* New York: DC Comics, 2007.

Sohn, Emily, Steve Erwin, and Charles Barnett. *A Crash Course in Forces and Motion with Max Axiom, Super Scientist.* Mankato, MN: Capstone Press, 2007.

Spiegelman, Art. *Maus: A Survivor's Tale.* New York: Pantheon Books, 1986.

Spiegelman, Art, and Françoise Mouly. *Big Fat Little Lit.* New York: Puffin, 2006.

Sturm, James, and Rich Tommaso. *Satchel Paige: Striking Out Jim Crow.* New York: Jump at the Sun, 2007.

Sugisaki, Yukiru. *D N Angel: Heart of Darkness.* Los Angeles, CA: Tokyopop, 2003.

Sugisaki, Yukiru. *D N Angel: Double Helix.* Los Angeles, CA: Tokyopop, 2004.

Sugisaki, Yukiru, Alethea Nibley, and Athena Nibley. *D N Angel: Facets of Darkness.* Los Angeles, CA: Tokyopop, 2004.

Sugisaki, Yukiru, Alethea Nibley, Athena Nibley, and Sarah Dyer. *D N Angel: Magical Girls.* Los Angeles, CA: Tokyopop, 2004.

Sugisaki, Yukiru, Alethea Nibley, Athena Nibley, and Sarah Dyer. *D N Angel: Dark Side of Love.* Los Angeles, CA: Tokyopop, 2004.

Takaya, Natsuki. *Fruits Basket: Volume 1.* Los Angeles, CA: Tokyopop, 2004.

Takaya, Natsuki. *Fruits Basket: Volume 2.* Los Angeles, CA: Tokyopop, 2004.

Takaya, Natsuki. *Fruits Basket: Volume 3.* Los Angeles, CA: Tokyopop, 2004.

Takaya, Natsuki. *Fruits Basket: Volume 4*. Los Angeles, CA: Tokyopop, 2004.
Takaya, Natsuki. *Fruits Basket: Volume 5*. Los Angeles, CA: Tokyopop, 2004.
Tan, Shaun. *The Arrival*. New York: Arthur A. Levine Books, 2007.
Telgemeier, Raina. *Smile*. New York: Graphix, 2010.
TenNapel, Doug. *Ghostopolis*. New York: Graphix/Scholastic, 2010.
Varon, Sara. *Robot Dreams*. New York: First Second, 2007.
Waid, Mark, and Leinil F. Yu. *Superman Birthright*. New York: DC Comics, 2004.
Wood, Don. *Into the Volcano: A Graphic Novel*. New York: The Blue Sky Press, 2008.
Yang, Gene L., and Lark Pien. *American Born Chinese*. New York: First Second, 2006.
Yolen, Jane, and Michael Cavallaro. *Foiled*. New York: First Second, 2010.

Appendix 2

Abadzis, Nick, and Hilary Sycamore. *Laika*. New York: First Second, 2007.

Abel, Jessica, Gabriel Soria, and Warren Pleece. *Life Sucks*. New York: First Second, 2008.

Anderson, Ho Che. *King: A Comics Biography of Martin Luther King, Jr.* Seattle, WA: Fantagraphics, 2005.

Arakawa, Hiromu. *Fullmetal Alchemist. Volume 1*. San Francisco, CA: Viz Media, LLC, 2006.

Arakawa, Hiromu. *Fullmetal Alchemist. Volume 2*. San Francisco, CA: Viz Media, LLC, 2006.

Arakawa, Hiromu. *Fullmetal Alchemist. Volume 3*. San Francisco, CA: Viz Media, LLC, 2006.

Arakawa, Hiromu. *Fullmetal Alchemist. Volume 4*. San Francisco, CA: Viz Media, LLC, 2006.

Arakawa, Hiromu. *Fullmetal Alchemist. Volume 5*. San Francisco, CA: Viz Media, LLC, 2006.

Busiek, Kurt, Alex Ross, and Richard Starkings. *Marvels*. New York: Marvel Publishing, 2008.

Busiek, Kurt. *Kurt Busiek's Astro City: Confession*. La Jolla CA: Homage Comics, 1997.

Busiek, Kurt. *Kurt Busiek's Astro City: Family Album*. La Jolla CA: Homage Comics, 1998.

Busiek, Kurt. *Kurt Busiek's Astro City: Life in the Big City*. La Jolla CA: Homage Comics, 1996.

Card, Orson S., Christopher Yost, Pasqual Ferry, Frank D'Armata, Cory Petit, and Jake Black. *Ender's Game: Battle School*. New York: Marvel Publishing Inc, 2009.

Dembicki, Matt. *Trickster: Native American Tales: A Graphic Collection*. Golden, CO: Fulcrum Pub., 2010.

Gaiman, Neil, Chris Bachalo, Michael Zulli, Steve Parkhouse, Mike Dringenberg, Malcolm Jones, Todd Klein, and John Costanza. *The Sandman: The Doll's House*. New York: DC Comics, 2010.

Gaiman, Neil, Kelley Jones, Malcolm Jones, Charles Vess, Colleen Doran, and Neil Gaiman. *The Sandman: Dream Country*. New York: Vertico/DC Comics, 2010.

Gaiman, Neil, Mike Dringenberg, Malcolm Jones, and Kelley Jones. *The Sandman: Season Mists*. New York: DC Comics, 2010.

Gaiman, Neil, Sam Kieth, Mike Dringenberg, Malcolm Jones, Todd Klein, Robbie Busch, Danny Vozzo, and Dave McKean. *The Sandman: Preludes & Nocturnes*. New York: DC Comics, 1995.

Gaiman, Neil, Shawn McManus, Todd Klein, Danny Vozzo, Dave McKean, and Samuel R. Delany. *The Sandman: A Game of You*. New York, NY: DC Comics, 1993.

Graphic Classics: O. Henry. Edited by Tom Pomplun. Graphic Classics Ser. Mounth Horeb, MI: Eureka Productions, 2005.

Guibert, Emmanuel. *Alan's War: The Memories of G.I. Alan Cope*. New York: First Second, 2008.

Guibert, Emmanuel, Didier Lefèvre, Frédéric Lemercier, and Alexis Siegel. *The Photographer*. New York: First Second, 2009.

Hamilton, Tim, and Ray Bradbury. *Ray Bradbury's Fahrenheit 451: The Authorized Adaptation*. New York: Hill and Wang, 2009.

Helfer, Andrew, and Randy DuBurke. *Malcolm X: A Graphic Biography*. New York: Hill and Wang, 2006.

Hennessey, Jonathan, and Aaron McConnell. *The United States Constitution: A Graphic Adaptation*. New York: Hill and Wang, 2008.

Hinds, Gareth. *Beowulf*. Cambridge, Mass: Candlewick Press, 2007.

Jacobson, Sid, Ernie Colón, Thomas H. Kean, and Lee Hamilton. *The 9/11 Report: A Graphic Adaptation*. New York: Hill and Wang, 2006.

Jones, Sabrina. *Isadora Duncan: A Graphic Biography*. New York: Hill and Wang, 2008.

Kim, Tong-hwa, Lauren Na, Min-ho Hwang, and Alexis Siegel. *The Color of Earth*. New York: First Second, 2009.

Kim, Young, and Stephenie Meyer. *Twilight: The Graphic Novel*. New York: Yen Press, 2010.

Kishimoto, Masashi, and Jo Duffy. *Naruto: The Tests of the Ninja*. San Francisco, CA: Viz, 2007.

Kishimoto, Masashi, and Jo Duffy. *Naruto: The Worst Client*. San Francisco, CA: Viz, 2007.

Kishimoto, Masashi, and Jo Duffy. *Naruto: Bridge of Courage*. San Francisco, CA: Viz, 2007.

Kishimoto, Masashi, and Jo Duffy. *Naruto: The Next Level*. San Francisco, CA: Viz, 2007.

Kishimoto, Masashi, and Jo Duffy. *Naruto: The Challengers*. San Francisco, CA: Viz, 2008.

Kouno, Fumiyo, Naoko Amemiya, and Andy Nakatani. *Town of Evening Calm, Country of Cherry Blossoms*. San Francisco, CA: Last Gasp, 2009.

Kubo, Tite, Lance Caselman, and Joe Yamazaki. *Bleach 1: Strawberry and the Soul Reapers*. San Francisco, CA: Viz, 2004.

Kubo, Tite, Lance Caselman, and Joe Yamazaki. *Bleach 2: Goodbye Parakeet, Good Night My Sister*. San Francisco, CA: Viz, 2004.

Kubo, Tite, and Lance Caselman. *Bleach 3: Memories in the Rain*. San Francisco, CA: Viz, 2004.

Kubo, Tite, and Lance Caselman. *Bleach 4: Quincy Archer Hates You*. San Francisco, CA: Viz, 2004.

Kubo, Tite, and Lance Caselman. *Bleach. 5: Right Arm of the Giant*. San Francisco, CA: Viz, 2006.

Larson, Hope. *Mercury*. New York: Atheneum Books for Young Readers, 2010.

Lee, Tony, Sam Hart, and Artur Fujita. *Outlaw: The Legend of Robin Hood, a Graphic Novel*. Somerville, MA: Candlewick Press, 2009.

Loeb, Jeph, Tim Sale, and Bob Kane. *Batman: The Long Halloween*. New York: DC Comics, 1998.

Love, Jeremy, and Patrick Morgan. *Bayou: Volume One*. New York: DC Comics, 2009.

McCloud, Scott. *Understanding Comics: The Invisible Art*. New York: Harper Perennial, 1994.

Medley, Linda, and Jane Yolen. *Castle Waiting: Volume 1*. Seattle, WA: Fantagraphics, 2006.

Miller, Frank. *Batman: The Dark Knight Returns*. New York: DC Comics, 2002.

Moore, Alan, Dave Gibbons, and John Higgins. *Watchmen*. New York: DC Comics, 2008.

Neri, Greg, and Randy DuBurke. *Yummy: The Last Days of a Southside Shorty*. New York: Lee & Low Books, 2010.

Neufeld, Josh. *A. D: New Orleans After the Deluge*. New York: Pantheon Books, 2009.

Novgorodoff, Danica, James Ponsoldt, Benjamin Percy, and Hilary Sycamore. *Refresh, Refresh: A Graphic Novel*. New York: First Second, 2009.

Ohba, Tsugumi. *Death Note 1: Boredom*. San Francisco, CA: VIZ Media, 2008.

Ohba, Tsugumi. *Death Note 2: Confluence*. San Francisco, CA: VIZ Media, 2008.

Ohba, Tsugumi. *Death Note 3: Hard Run*. San Francisco, CA: VIZ Media, 2008.

Ohba, Tsugumi. *Death Note 4: Love*. San Francisco, CA: VIZ Media, 2008.

Ohba, Tsugumi. *Death Note 5: Whiteout*. San Francisco, CA: VIZ Media, 2008.

Ottaviani, Jim. *Fallout: J. Robert Oppenheimer, Leo Szilard, and the Political Science of the Atomic Bomb*. Ann Arbor, MI: G.T. Labs, 2001.

Pink, Daniel H, and Pas R. Ten. *The Adventures of Johnny Bunko: The Last Career Guide You'll Ever Need*. New York: Riverhead Books, 2008.

Poe, Marshall, and Ellen Lindner. *Little Rock Nine*. New York: Aladdin Paperbacks, 2008.

Porcellino, John. *Thoreau at Walden*. New York: Hyperion Books, 2008.

Renier, Aaron, and Alec Longstreth. *The Unsinkable Walker Bean*. New York: First Second, 2010.

Satrapi, Marjane. *Persepolis*. New York: Pantheon Books, 2003.

Schultz, Mark, Zander Cannon, and Kevin Cannon. *The Stuff of Life: A Graphic Guide to Genetics and DNA*. New York: Hill and Wang, 2009.

Sfar, Joann, Antoine de Saint-Exupéry, and Brigitte Findakly. *The Little Prince*. Boston: Houghton Mifflin Harcourt. 2010.

Shakespeare, William. *The Merchant of Venice*. Adapted and illustrated by Gareth Hinds. MA: Candlewick Press. 2008.

Shakespeare, William. *Romeo and Juliet: The Graphic Novel*. Adapted by Jon McDonald and illustrated by Will Volley, et al. Towcester, UK: Classical Comics, 2009.

Shivack, Nadia. *Inside Out: Portrait of an Eating Disorder*. New York: Atheneum Books for Young Readers, 2007.

Sina, A. B., LeUyen Pham, Alex Puvilland, and Jordan Mechner. *Prince of Persia, the Graphic Novel*. New York: First Second, 2008.

Small, David. *Stitches: A Memoir —*. New York: W.W. Norton & Co, 2009.

Smith, Jeff, and Steve Hamaker. *Bone: Out from Boneville*. New York: Graphix/Scholastic, 2005.

Smith, Jeff, and Steve Hamaker. *Bone: The Great Cow Race*. New York: Graphix/Scholastic, 2005.

Smith, Jeff, and Steve Hamaker. *Bone: Eyes of the Storm*. New York: Graphix/Scholastic, 2006.

Smith, Jeff, and Steve Hamaker. *Bone: The Dragon Slayer*. New York: Graphix/Scholastic, 2006.

Smith, Jeff, and Steve Hamaker. *Bone: Rock Jaw Master of the Eastern Border*. New York: Graphix/Scholastic, 2007.

Spiegelman, Art. *Maus: A Survivor's Tale*. New York: Pantheon Books, 1986.

Takahashi, Rumiko. *Ranma 1/2: Vol. 1*. San Francisco, CA: Viz Communications, 2003.

Takahashi, Rumiko. *Ranma 1/2: Vol. 2*. San Francisco, CA: Viz Communications, 2003.

Takahashi, Rumiko. *Ranma 1/2: Vol. 3*. San Francisco, CA: Viz Communications, 2003.

Takahashi, Rumiko. *Ranma 1/2: Vol. 4*. San Francisco, CA: Viz Communications, 2003.

Takahashi, Rumiko. *Ranma 1/2: Vol. 5*. San Francisco, CA: Viz Communications, 2003.

Takaya, Natsuki. *Fruits Basket: Volume 1*. Los Angeles, CA: Tokyopop, 2004.

Takaya, Natsuki. *Fruits Basket: Volume 2*. Los Angeles, CA: Tokyopop, 2004.

Takaya, Natsuki. *Fruits Basket: Volume 3*. Los Angeles, CA: Tokyopop, 2004.

Takaya, Natsuki. *Fruits Basket: Volume 4*. Los Angeles, CA: Tokyopop, 2004.

Takaya, Natsuki. *Fruits Basket: Volume 5*. Los Angeles, CA: Tokyopop, 2004.

Tamaki, Mariko, and Jillian Tamaki. *Skim*. Toronto: Groundwood Books, 2008.

Tan, Shaun. *The Arrival*. New York: Arthur A. Levine Books, 2007.

Vaughan, Brian K., Niko Henrichon, and Todd Klein. *Pride of Baghdad*. New York: DC Comics, 2006.

Whedon, Joss, and John Cassaday. *Astonishing X-Men: Vol. 1 Gifted*. New York: Marvel Comics, 2004.

Whedon, Joss, and John Cassaday. *Astonishing X-Men: Vol. 2 Dangerous*. New York: Marvel Comics, 2005.

Whedon, Joss, and John Cassaday. *Astonishing X-Men: Vol. 3 Torn*. New York: Marvel Comics, 2007.

Whedon, Joss, and John Cassaday. *Astonishing X-Men: Vol. 4 Unstoppable.* New York: Marvel Comics, 2008.

White, Tracy. *How I Made It to Eighteen: A Mostly True Story.* New York: Roaring Brook Press, 2010.

Wilson, G. W., and M. K. Perker. *Cairo: A Graphic Novel.* New York: DC Comics, 2007.

Winick, Judd. *Pedro and Me: Friendship, Loss, and What I Learned.* New York: Henry Holt, 2000.

Yang, Gene L., and Lark Pien. *American Born Chinese.* New York: First Second, 2006.

Yang, Gene L., and Derek K. Kim. *The Eternal Smile: Three Stories.* New York: First Second, 2009.

Yolen, Jane, and Michael Cavallaro. *Foiled.* New York: First Second, 2010.

Zimmerman, Dwight J., and Wayne Vansant. *The Vietnam War: A Graphic History.* New York: Hill and Wang, 2009.

Index

About the Authors

KAREN W. GAVIGAN is an assistant professor in the School of Library and Information Science at the University of South Carolina in Columbia, SC. Dr. Gavigan's research interests include the use of graphic novels with struggling male adolescent readers.

MINDY TOMASEVICH is a media specialist and National Board Certified Teacher at Mills Park Middle School in Cary, NC.